JONI MITCHELL

PAVED PARADISE

Paul Barrera

AGENDA, ANDOVER, HAMPSHIRE, U.K.

Published by
Agenda Ltd, Units 1 & 2, Ludgershall Business Park,
New Drove, Andover, Hampshire, U.K., SP11 9RN

Paved Paradise
Paul Barrera

First Published October 1998

For Cathy Foulkes

British Library Cataloguing in Publication Data.
A catalogue record for this book is available from the British Library

All rights reserved, no parts of this publication may be reproduced stored in a retrieval system, or transmitted, in any form or by any means, electronic, mechanical, photocopying, recording or otherwise, without the prior permission of Agenda Limited.

Copyright Agenda Ltd 1998

ISBN 1 899882 85 5

CONTENTS

SONG TO A SEAGULL.... 10

CLOUDS.... 23

LADIES OF THE CANYON.... 29

BLUE.... 39

FOR THE ROSES.... 45

COURT AND SPARK.... 50

MILES OF AISLES.... 55
HISSING OF SUMMER LAWNS

HEJIRA.... 63

DON JUAN'S RESTLESS DAUGHTER.... 68

MINGUS.... 74

SHADOWS AND LIGHT.... 81
WILD THINGS RUN FAST

DOG EAT DOG.... 88
CHALK MARK IN A RAINSTORM

NIGHT RIDE HOME.... 97
TURBULENT INDIGO

GHOSTS.... 107
HITS/MISSES

TAMING THE TIGER.... 111

TRACK FINDER.... 118

ACKNOWLEDGEMENTS.... 122

Joni Mitchell

INTRODUCTION

The lot of a critic is to be remembered by what he failed to understand.
George Moore (1852-1933)

I have always been a fan of Joni Mitchell's music, I have not always been a fan of her frankness and outspoken behaviour. For many years her work received no publicity, hardly any radio-plays and in some cases no promotion except for record reviews. I realise that this can be misconstrued as an overstatement but Joni does feel that she was shut-out of the industry for a long period of time. To equalise the facts one has to bear in mind that Joni would regularly say in interviews that she was retiring, or the latest album would be her last as she wanted to devote more of her time to painting. There are many musicians that are also painters, Bob Dylan, Ron Wood and of course Don van Vliet, a.k.a. Captain Beefheart. Vliet gave up the music business completely on his realisation that to be accepted as an artist and sculptor one needs to concentrate totally on the route one intends to take. Joni could never quite make up her mind, my opinion is that she preferred painting but needed the accolades that music brings and the financial rewards. She realised that she would not be in a position to support her lifestyle by painting alone, she was in a Catch-22 situation of her own creation.

Joni has become an accomplished painter of that there is no doubt. Some of her cover paintings seem to be a little wayward on perspective but the 'Turbulent Indigo' album for which she would win an award for her designs is superb. I would think that winning that award gave her a great deal of pleasure and encouragement. Just as her home in Saskatchewan and Canada has appeared in her songs it is also an important subject for her paintings. The area to the north of the Canadian State where Joni was brought up is known for having magnificent skies, red pepper coloured sands, open-spaces, sand-storms, and in Winter snow and ice, providing the opportunity to skate on frozen lakes and ponds and observe the distant snow capped mountains. All these changes are set beside the small town activities and attitudes of the area such as the grocery store and the regular gossip that occurs there. Joni has stretched her sights out to the largest of cities but was always homesick for the peace and tranquillity; yet she is always anxious about loneliness, it is an eternal problem for gregarious people, it is all there in her songs.

In her recent interview for Mojo Magazine Joni talked to Dave DiMartino. Joni said that she disliked and resented people picking the songs apart and saying who they thought the song concerned. Well that could be easily corrected if she actually wrote the correct information after each song, or alternatively said the name of the person in the song. Her word 'resent' almost implies that the songs are 'hers' written for 'her' and the people who pay the money for the records have no rights whatsoever, I find myself at loggerheads with her by implication. Bob Dylan has never bothered to confirm or deny any of the analysis of his lyrics, it adds to the mystery. If critics like me get it all wrong, and subsequently I am incorrect in the pages of this book then so-be-it, nothing is known for certain, it is all alleged and it is basically my working hypothesis. Joni admits to 'taking pages from her life' and making them into songs, many are obvious, especially the songs for her parents and daughter.

When she is in love the album shows that fact, when she feels lost and forgotten that is also portrayed. If she does not want our analysis then she should only record other writer's songs and nursery rhymes, the analysis to my mind adds to the power and interest of the songs rather than detracts or diminishes them in any way. To placate Joni's attack on the critics I add here that all my opinions are assumptions, no more, no less. I am also not sure how 'my' naming the protagonist in any song can embarrass Joni, all she has to say is 'It is not about him or alternatively it is 'X'', and thus the debate is closed.

At the time of my writing this book Joni is 55 years old, looks 45, she continues to sing in live shows, paints pictures, writes songs and enjoys the company of men whilst continuing to live dangerously by smoking cigarettes. The smoking may be part of her need to do something that presents her original 'wild child of the 1960s' persona. She always appeared to be delicate and vulnerable when inside that delightful frame she was as strong as anyone that had grown up in the wilds of Canada. Myrtle Joni's mother whose life is the object of some of Joni's songs is now a formidable 86 years old.

Although Joni has always chosen to be private her songs are part of her life, many writers before me have given their opinions of her songs and the protagonists within them, my attempts are given with all my best intentions. What one must remember is, I, like so many others judge myself by my best intentions and others by their worst actions. Persons that have given their whole life over to charity, public life or other selfless practices continue to be pilloried for a single indiscretion, I hope that in this book I make no profound judgements, only inferences.

Joni continues to enthral and antagonise. I can still remember the first time I saw her. She was apparently nervous, that high voice full of tremolo and trepidation. Suddenly she turned to the audience and smiled, it was just as though the sun had come out. The teeth take up nearly all of her face, the eyes become narrow, she becomes even more beautiful and susceptible, the audience just wants her to succeed, they will forgive her everything, providing they can hear her, we could and we did.

Joni shares her birthday with trumpeter Al Hirt, singer Dee Clark and Johnny Rivers. They are all older than Joni as is Mary Travers the blonde 'Mary' who was sandwiched between Peter and Paul singing 'Leaving on a Jet Plane', a song with a similar subject would be composed by Joni later in her career. I only make these birthday comparison because Joni is aware that she was born with 'Scorpio Rising' as were (indicated by Brian Hinton) John Milton and Sigmund Freud. Joni played her part in attempting to obtain for her generation that chance of achieving that elusive dream, they were the love generation, the dream fluttered away just like Bob Lind's elusive butterfly.

Joni has never sidestepped controversy, self understanding pours from her written work, her private life has been the subject of much unscrupulous journalism, this has conspired to make her stronger and more resilient than ever. She often reaches out to her adopted daughter in song, in Joni's opinion she did so to soften the blow of deep felt loss.

In my opinion she is yet to make a poor album, some lacked a decent tune but the lyrics compensated, one album was one of the greatest (if not the greatest) live show by a female artist. I hope that you join me on this trip down nostalgia lane, I also hope that if you have not been a lover of her music or ego that you try again. I make no apologies for my views in this book, I repeat that they are all given with an honesty which may be at odds with your ideas. If I make you listen to a couple of album tracks again and you decided that I might be correct then I have achieved the object of this track-by-track evaluation. Joni has recently released her 17th album, it is 31 years since her first album, and it all seemed like it was only yesterday.

Paul Barrera
1998

JONI MITCHELL (Song to a Seagull) 1968

*The singer must have the universal ground of all mood,
the ability to apply imagination to the voice,
the ability to sing with imagination.*

Soren Kierkegaad (1813-1855)

Myrtle Marguerite McKee was a thirty year old school teacher working in a Bank in a town named Regina, in Saskatchewan State, Canada. It was 1942 all the able bodied men were serving in the army on active service in World War II. With so few men around Myrtle had a blind-date arranged with a serving Air Force Man, an instructor named William Anderson. It was love at first sight, Myrtle said the reason was that he looked so dashing in his uniform and she found him irresistible. They travelled fifty miles to Moose Jaw (or more likely to Medicine Hat, 400 miles away in the next State Alberta), where they were married. Timothy White in his book 'Rock Lives - Profiles and Interviews' explained the intricacies of the story. Apparently Myrtle had visited a gypsy who had read her the leaves in her tea-cup. The gypsy informed a surprised and incredulous Myrtle that she would be married within a month and have a child within a year. The gypsy added that Myrtle would also die a long and agonizing death, two of the predictions came true, the third hopefully remains unlikely, Myrtle is alive and well and 86 years of age. Because at the time all the available men were away on military duty Myrtle gave no credence to the fortune-telling; Myrtle's daughter Joan would write a song 'The Tea Leaf Prophecy' of that gypsy in 1988.

Myrtle's family were homesteaders living in Creelman, Saskatchewan, William Anderson's father was a Norwegian immigrant also named William. Myrtle's father James McKee was an pioneering Irish farmer who built a small house so that he could make a claim and thus be entitled to an allotment of government land. James' wife Sadie McKee was later name checked on Joni Mitchell's second album 'Clouds'. William and Myrtle set up home in Canadian Air Force Quarters, they had little or no privacy and at times lived in a large room with another couple with the living quarters only separated by a hanging curtain. The Gypsy's second prophecy of a child born within a year came true and Roberta Joan Anderson was born on November 7th, 1943 at Fort McLeod, Alberta, Canada. Apparently Joan's parents had expected her to be a boy so her name was a slight change to the anticipated Robert John. Joni is a Scorpio, and it has been often mentioned that she was born at the time designated as Scorpio-Rising, (as was Neil Young another Canadian born two years after Joni). It is stated in the astrology charts that persons born at this time in the astrological galactic calendar are extremely resilient and are able to face problems as they happen and gain strength by over-coming them. Joan's family still were unsettled and they moved onto Calgary, in Alberta State, there they again lived in one room. They did not stay there for long, soon they were on the road again settling for a while in Saskatoon in the Canadian prairie, then Joan's family moved on to North Battleford eighty miles north of Saskatoon where Joan went to school from the age of six. There seems some confusion over another place of residence; Yorkton is 200 miles from Saskatoon, but there is a Yorkville in Yorktown near Toronto, where Joni lived later in her life. The latitude of Canada's populated areas would compare in England with Sunderland in the North and Exeter in the South, this is probably the reason why Toronto was so popular being as far South as Canada stretched, Toronto had less severe winters.

Life after the war was difficult especially as there were shortages of everything. In an interview for 'Q' Magazine Joan recalled how wonderful it was when soap suddenly became available, even socks were difficult to buy. Joan suffered from German Measles, Red Measles, Scarlet Fever, Appendicitis, tonsillitis, Chicken Pox, as if this wasn't enough at the age of nine she was struck down in the 1952 Canadian polio epidemic, this also struck down Neil Young. Joan had burning pains in her spine which she would later mention in a song. Joan gained her strength in the face of adversity as predicted by the stars, the illness left her with a twisted spine. At least she and Neil Young survived when so many others died.

Joan's family were not musical in fact she explained to Dave DiMartino in Mojo Magazine that they had only a few records in the house. Bill had records by Harry James and Leroy Anderson, both trumpet players, and Myrtle had 'Clair De Lune' and 'Brahms Lullaby', records were expensive and of course at that time made of shellac which was extremely fragile.

Joan stated in an interview that she could remember a coloured roll-up blind that was suspended over her crib, in fact she said that it was dark green. After Joan was released from hospital to convalesce from polio, Myrtle used her teaching skills to tutor Joan at home. Joan was a quick learner and by the age of twelve was regularly travelling to town alone. She was dress size-8 which was the size that clothes salesmen needed for models to parade their latest designed dresses to the shops. Joan became a model for the salesmen when they arrived in Saskatoon.

Joan had seen the film 'The Tales of Hoffmann' in 1952, which starred Robert Helpmann, Robert Rounseville, Pamela Brown and Moira Shearer. The film was in fact three adventures of the Poet Hoffmann, he is seeking the eternal woman and is beset by eternal evil. What so impressed young Joan was the scene where the alchemist transforms wax into jewels. Joan was aware at a very early age how colours change and merge and she was soon drawing and painting for pleasure. Joan had a natural drawing ability, a gift.

Joan attended classes at Queen Elizabeth Public School and then moved on to Nutana and Aden Bowan High Schools. She was continuing to model clothes in Saskatoon and saving the money so that she could one day in the future send herself to Art School. Her academic achievements were not good, she was becoming more interested in painting, she realised she had a natural aptitude. Her school art teacher's name was Henry Bonli and because she liked the way his name looked as a signature on his paintings she decided to change her name from Joan to Joni. Joni was to have her first claim to fame in her home town not for painting or from music, in fact she was yet to show much interest in music, but she enjoyed dancing. She had been friends with a young man who played the organ at the local church, it seems that he was instrumental in first whetting the musical taste buds of young Joni. But to return to her claim to early fame.

Johnny Cash was an emerging talent, he had a No 1 hit in America at the time with 'Teenage Queen'. As a promotional concept Cash went from town to town on his musical tour crowning a teenage queen in each town. Joni entered but sadly only came second, then fate took a hand. The girl that was selected as the winner suddenly died so Joni in second place became The Teenage Queen of Saskatoon, and she was crowned by Johnny Cash.

Joni considered treating herself to a guitar and teaching herself to play it. Myrtle objected, she thought that the guitar was solely connected with Country and Western Music, a style she hated, she couldn't be convinced that it was also a folk music instrument. Joni spent her hard earned modelling money on a baritone ukulele, it cost $36.

Joni then bought her first album for playing on the family gramophone. It was the Lambert, Hendricks and Ross album 'Hottest New Sound in Jazz'. It was a matter of hours before Joni could scat-sing along with Annie Ross on the wonderful jazz vocalese songs. Jon Hendricks, Eddie Jefferson and King Pleasure, were adding lyrics to many of the quality jazz solos that were in abundance at the time. The LHR album that Joni had bought included 'Twisted' (written by Annie Ross, in 1952) a song that Joni would eventually record herself. Joni learned to play the ukulele from a Pete Seeger instruction record and the accompanying tutor manual. She managed to get a job playing at The Louis Riel, a cafe in Saskatoon, with the money she earned singing folk songs she bought her first guitar.

At the age of 20 Joni found that she was pregnant, although it is an accepted fact of life nowadays that children are born to single unmarried parents, back in 1963 the stigma against such a thing happening was strong. The all encompassing opinion of the day was that all pregnant girls were loose harlots. Joni decided to have the child and a daughter named Kelly was born, because of the situation of the day she had the child adopted, this has been a continuing sadness throughout Joni's life and the feeling of forfeiture often occurs in her song lyrics. It is pertinent that if she had retained the child then she would not have become a singer-songwriter.

In 1963 Joni went back to Calgary and enrolled in the Alberta College of Art. She soon became despondent and disillusioned with the style of teaching. Joni realised that she had to learn the basics first before finding her own style. The pretentious teachers were more interested in expressionism and the abstract arts, Joni wanted realism first. This is all the more strange when one understands that Joni had actually enrolled in a commercial artist course. All artists have to 'pay their dues', it is the same with jazz musicians, they have to learn and prove that they can play standard scales and songs before they can sweep off onto long meandering honk and squawk solos. Before Jackson Pollock was dribbling paint over a canvas he was painting portraits and landscapes, the same must be said for all the great artists.

Joni was continuing her studies at Art College, she was now playing a guitar and singing at the local Calgary night spot 'The Depression', she was earning $15 for a weekend, every little helped a struggling art student. The owner of The Depression was John Uhren he was paying for various other Canadian folk singers to play at the club. Peter Albing (sometimes spelled, Albling) and Joni became the house musicians. Joni already had her trademark, her long blonde hair, John Uhren was convinced that she was bringing in the customers. Joni decided to travel for three days via The Canadian Pacific Railroad to Toronto to attend the 1964 Mariposa Folk Festival. It was at the festival that she finally decided to be singer rather than a painter. Joni was of course in good company deciding to leave Art School. One of her main influences was Vincent Van Gogh, he was rarely taught anything, in fact he wrote letters to his friends (particularly Bernard) pleading for them to cease their art tuition so that they could express themselves through their art rather than be tainted by the views and styles of others. Joni decided on a similar course, play music and teach-herself art, at least the final product would be from her heart.

She never returned to Art College she went to Yorkville in Yorktown, the area populated by the aesthetes of Toronto. This area was the equivalent of Greenwich Village, or perhaps Soho in London, cosmopolitan and artistically educational. Joni had completed her first song composition namely 'Day After Day', as far as I can ascertain it has never been recorded. In Yorkville, Buffy Sainte-Marie a Cree Indian who had lived on an Indian Reservation close to Saskatoon was singing, also the emerging protest singer Phil Ochs and Blood Sweat and Tears singer David Clayton Thomas were also performing in the local clubs, as were Jose Feliciano and John Kay's Steppenwolf. Canada also had poet Leonard Cohen, (he was not yet singing) and Gordon Lightfoot who was already recording, Lightfoot had the style of a more melodic but less political Bob Dylan.

Joni Anderson got a gig singing in the basement of The Penny Farthing Folk Club, it was here that she was to meet Chuck Mitchell. The Penny Farthing Club had a superior upstairs club for the more affluent customers, Chuck Mitchell had been contracted to sing for them. The payment for working the club basement was insufficient to support Joni so she worked during the day a shop assistant. This salesgirl lifestyle was a means to an end, she needed to raise $140 to pay for membership to the Musicians Union, she was really playing at The Penny Farthing illegally. Joni was living in a communal hostel at the time so she was pleased to have a friend in Chuck Mitchell. The couple became closer and they were married in June 1965 in Michigan. Chuck, seven years Joni's senior, actually offered to take in Joni's daughter, but she was already living with her new adoptive parents. Joni and Chuck set up home in Detroit just across the bay from Toronto but now they were living in The U.S.A. Their house became a hostel for itinerant musicians, Gordon Lightfoot, Buffy Sainte-Marie, David Blue, Tom Rush and many others stayed at times. Joni and Chuck worked as a duo around the North American circuit and did reasonably well. They also went to New York and played The Gaslight Club, this gig was the highlight of their career as a partnership. Chuck considered himself a musical academic and his wife Joni was just an amateur. As Joni was now writing some good songs Chuck had trouble accepting that he was fast becoming the junior partner in the act, in fact it drove a wedge between them and they soon separated. Whilst working at a club called the Riverboat, Joni was asked to write a theme song for The Canadian Broadcasting Company, the resulting song was titled 'The Way It Is'. Gordon Lightfoot would later record a song called 'The Way I Feel', and be asked to write a song called 'The Canadian Railroad Trilogy' for film. Bruce Hornsby also wrote and recorded 'The Way It Is', it is not Joni's song.

Joni was becoming quite well known in New York. Her friendship with Tom Rush was ultimately to assist her career considerably. Joni was singing at the Checkmate Club in Detroit and Tom Rush admired her compositions 'Urge For Going' and 'Tin Angel so much that he adopted them into his act and later recorded them. Apparently 'Urge for Going' had been offered to Judy Collins who had declined the song. Tom Rush released 'The Circle Game' (also a Joni Mitchell song, written for Neil Young) Album in 1968, he had recorded three folk blues albums previously, this was his second for Jac Holzman's Elektra. Tom Rush continued to give Joni the encouragement she needed, Chuck Mitchell never gave her the re-assurance and motivation. Joni sang at New York's Gaslight Club again and decided to re-locate to Manhattan, she settled in a one room apartment in the Chelsea district.

Joni was now beginning to earn some good money, she received B.M.I. royalties for the songs she had written and was getting plenty of professional engagements. She had been managing her own affairs until she met Elliot Roberts who became her manager. His first professional advice was that Joni should form her own music publishing company and 'Siquomb Music' was born. Siquomb is an acronym for 'She is Queen Un-disputedly of Mind Beauty', but it is my guess that this was actually created afterwards from the name. It could in fact be phonetic for 'seek-them' or 'succumb', bearing in mind that 'siouan' is the language spoken by Sioux Red Indians. There is however another acronym in a title on Joni's first album in the song titled 'Sisotowbell Lane'. The forming of her own publishing company remains one of the masterpieces of sound management advice ever given to Joni, before 1970 was out her publishing company was valued at $1.5 million, it remains in position to care for Joni in her dotage.

Joni's songs were becoming sought after, 'Clouds' (later re-titled 'Both Sides Now') was recorded by gruff singing folk singer Dave Van Ronk. Judy Collins on her 1967 'Wildflowers' album included 'Michael of the Mountains' and 'Both Sides Now'. Buffy Sainte-Marie recorded 'Circle Game' and 'Ode

(Song) to A Seagull', all these recordings were before Joni recorded her own versions. Elliot Roberts suggested that Joni should visit England, she travelled to London where she met Joe Boyd then managing (amongst others) The Incredible String Band. Joni had made some home tapes of some of her songs which were heard and later recorded by the top English female folk singer at the time, Julie Felix. The emerging folk group 'Fairport Convention' recorded 'Chelsea Morning' and 'I Don't Know Where I Stand' for their first album and put 'Eastern Rain' on their second album which was titled 'What We Did on Our Holidays'. 'Eastern Rain' has never been available by Joni herself except on a bootleg release. Joni had joined The Fairport Convention in their concert at The London Festival Hall. She met Sandy Denny (who replaced Judy Dyble in Fairport) and her then boyfriend Jackson C.Frank. Soon after this meeting Jackson C. Frank disappeared from the music scene and was not located again, living as a down-and-out, until 1992.

It was now 1968 and with Joni living in London she was an obvious choice to appear on top disc jockey John Peel's programme, Top Gear. According to Ken Garner's wonderful book 'In Session Tonight' he states that Joni Mitchell appeared on the programme on 29th September 1968. She sang, 'Chelsea Morning', 'Galleries' (Gallery?), 'Night in the City', and 'Cactus Tree'. The tracks were recorded on 23rd September. The backing group selected for the performance was excellent comprising Harold McNair on Saxophone, Danny Thompson on bass, John Cameron on piano, and Tony Carr on drums. Joni was contracted to provide other performances for The B.B.C. Radio One Club but she would later cancel all the dates.

On returning to America Joni settled in Los Angeles where she became very close to Motorhead Sherwood a member of Frank Zappa's Mothers of Invention band. Motorhead was the good looking lead performer in Frank's art-house movie '200 Motels', this was another relationship that was not to last. Joni was contracted to sing at The Coconut Grove in Florida where she was seen and heard by ex-Byrd David Crosby. Crosby had left The Byrds at the time they were recording 'The Notorious Byrd Brothers' album, on that album cover you can see that David Crosby has been substituted by a horse. When Joni returned to Los Angeles David Crosby offered his services as producer for her first album.

David and Joni become romantically attached and she was introduced to ex-Buffalo Springfield guitarist Stephen Stills, now a friend of Crosby. Manager Elliot Roberts was trying to get the best recording deal for Joni, he turned down folk label Vanguard that was promoting Joan Baez at the time and settled with Frank Sinatra's Reprise Records. Mo Ostin at Reprise Records wanted to hear a demonstration recording first and this was duly recorded. Mo Ostin liked what he heard and Joni had a record deal. Meanwhile Elliot Roberts also became the manager for Neil Young.

Joni Mitchell was to be sold to the listeners as the female equivalent to Bob Dylan, strangely in later years they would become members of a rare band of musician-painters who designed their own album sleeves. In fact Bob Dylan designed the sleeve for The Band's 'Music From Big Pink (1968)' before he did his own 'Self Portrait' and 'Planet Waves' albums.

JONI MITCHELL, SONG FOR A SEAGULL (released September 1968)

Although the album was produced by David Crosby he stated later that he had little to do with the album except for arranging Stephen Stills to play bass, Lee Keefer added some 'banshee' according to the cover, which I assume is an extra backing vocal. The album has always had two titles but this is because critics and fans alike did not look carefully enough at the cover design. The design is a sepia ink drawing by Joni with large areas painted in, like an half finished painting-by-numbers picture. A photograph on the rear shows Joni standing next to a red van which has been parked on the side-walk, she appears to be carrying her ukulele it seems much too small to be a guitar. She is sheltering from the rain under a red umbrella. As the first side of the album is sub-titled 'I Came to the City' one assumes that this actually is meant to depict Joni arriving. The photographer has taken the photograph from under his own green umbrella. The front cover has a second picture, much smaller in diameter, here the cameraman is laying on the ground aiming the camera upwards at Joni. From this small picture a swirl of colour descends into a peacock looking towards the left. As the gatefold opens flowers carry the eye across the page into the tail of a second peacock that is staring straight at Joni in the second picture. There are flowers, cacti and tresses of blonde hair which billow out containing the name 'Joni Mitchell'. The album title is written out in the seagull's formation to the right of the cover under Joni's printed name. The seagulls are flying up the cover from the sunset (or sunrise) over a sailing ship. As so few people actually saw the title written in the flying seagulls the album became known as the eponymous 'Joni Mitchell'.

The music contained therein is a good first album by anyone's standards, a folky album of self composed songs. The lyrics written out in the gatefold make way for a lovely photograph of Joni. The first side is titled 'I Came to the City', the second side 'Out of the City and Down to the Seaside'. Van Morrison had left his group 'Them' to go solo and was in the studio recording for 'Bang Records', he released 'Astral Weeks' after Joni's album and he also titled each side of that album inferring that the tracks were in a specific sequence. Joni's album was dedicated to her english literature teacher Mr Kratzmann, Joni adds in her sleeve notes 'who taught me to love words'.

I CAME TO THE CITY

I HAD A KING: A song written about the relationship with her estranged husband Chuck Mitchell. This of course is the first song that we ever heard from Joni, probably the best first track on any first album ever. She is immediately sharing with us her innermost feelings, she would exorcise her ghosts in songs for the rest of her career, what was startling was to hear this quality of poetry and music from such a young emerging singer. When she was married she was living in 'loves enchantment'. Chuck Mitchell was originally her knight in shining armour who had arrived on his white horse to love and protect her. Sadly, as so often happens, the dreams disappeared, the love turned away and evaporated, he just criticised. At least this mature lyric indicates in the last verse that there is no one to blame, and no one to name. When one lover leaves, the other partner changes the locks on the doors and their heart so that they can't get back in. So Joni commits regicide in a song, it was also proposed by another author that writer John Milton (as you may remember was also born a 'scorpio-rising'), also wrote of regicide, yet I think that was onerously applied to the plot of Milton's book 'Lycidas'. The monody of Milton's poem is mourning the death of one Edward King, he was a friend of Milton's that had drowned, not a 'King' at all except in name. Joni manages to explain so much in her short song, less than three minutes for this beautiful pure voice to make all the male listeners want to run to her and become her protecting hero. Joni would find more 'Kings' to take Chuck Mitchell's place in the coming years.

MICHAEL FROM THE MOUNTAINS: A song that probably influenced British folk singer Ralph McTell, he recorded a song 'Michael in the Garden' for his 'My Side of Your Window' album in 1969. I read in a review at the time that perhaps Joni had heard Ralph's song sung by Ralph when she was in England. Whatever the truth the songs are on different themes only the name in the title are identical, both songs are excellent. Ralph's Michael is set in 'Woodstock's' garden and Joni would later compose her own song for the site of 'Woodstock' referring to Yasgur's field as a garden. Joni's Michael is a childhood romance, Joni continues in the song to provide us with clues. Michael brings Sweets, they walk together in the rain, they go to a park, they have their paintings on the wall, their parents complain when they come home late, however do they go upstairs and dry 'each other' with towels? One wonders if this Michael might be the father of Joni's 'Kelly'. A beautiful gentle song of innocence. I read a review that stated that this Michael was mentally ill, that must have been Ralph McTell's Michael, not Joni's.

NIGHT IN THE CITY: Joni sings this song in a deeper voice and she sounds very similar to Joan Baez, the bass playing is courtesy of Stephen Stills. Joni is playing her plangent bar-room style piano, this bouncy ingenuous song has a superb descant on the echo vocal in the chorus; Joni considers this song to be a childlike ditty. Joseph Addison wrote in 1711 that 'Nothing is capable of being well set to music that is not nonsense'; I'm not sure I agree, but this is the song on the album that makes the casual listener sit up and take notice. A great song by any writer's standards, so catchy it can be sung on first hearing. A song for a nocturnal person that adores the night-life. Most musicians work night-hours anyway but here Joni views the song from a day worker whose life gains so much as soon as darkness falls. The night looks pretty, music spills into the street, and colours flash.....take the town by surprise!

MARCIE: This song of loneliness reminds me of Scott Walker's third album cunningly titled 'Scott 3'. Scott had detailed the loneliness of 'Rosemary' and 'Big Louise' and the stay-at-home-and-hope scenario in 'It's Raining Today'. 'Marcie' is a lonely woman waiting for a letter to arrive. She is filling her time by working around the house, but looks out of the window watching the postman hoping that there is a letter for her. Marcie goes to theatres on her own, walks in the snow and rain, dresses in a coat of flowers. She dreams back to her summer romance that is dead and gone. Sadly she buys a one way ticket and leaves her memories behind. This might be influenced by Leonard Cohen's 'So Long Marianne' or perhaps his 'Suzanne'. Joni uses the yellow cab and a faucet in her lyrics for the first time here, they would be used again.

NATHAN LA FRANEER: The title is presumed to the name of a taxi driver, it was written on his name plate within the cab. The track is sequenced perfectly so that Joni is now leaving the city and completing the side of the album dedicated to the urban environment. As she leaves in the yellow cab she describes the nightmare world she views from the cab window. She is in a hurry to escape the confines of suburbia but the driver takes her slowly as if in a slow motion film excerpt. Dear Nathan the taxi driver asks for an extra tip which is refused and he curses Joni to her face. This proves what she has said in the earlier part of the song, everybody is hustling something, the ageing hippie is now selling Superman balloons, everyone is grasping in this growing ghostly garden which was once filled with love.

OUT OF THE CITY AND DOWN TO THE SEASIDE

SISOTOWBELL LANE: The title of the song as mentioned earlier is an acronym. It means...Somehow In Spite Of Trouble Ours Will Be Ever Lasting Love. The sentiments are that away from the hectic pace of the city one can sit in a rocking chair and see the city, the badlands which are now far in the distance. Other writers have read so much into this lyric but for me it is just pastoral, a slowing down, a gentle and sensitive return to what a country girl would consider home.

THE DAWNTREADER: Joni has always had an artists eye for colours and collected coloured glass, here the lyric opens with 'Peridots' which are pieces of pale green transparent chrysolite which are often used as gem stones. 'Periwinkles' are of course edible shellfish, but they are also evergreen plants with trailing stems and blue flowers like medallions. So in five words in the kaleidoscopic first line we have gems and seashells or more likely gems and blue flowers. The song is an addition to the feelings presented by Sisotowbell Lane, the renewing of each day by the dawn, the gradual reawakening of colours. The sunlight will change the white city skin to a golden promise. Joni obviously loves to be by the sea, she can hear the tinkling of the rigging in the boats...sea-dreams.

THE PIRATE OF PENANCE: Is a song with two characters in a question and answer format. We have 'Penance Crane' a lady, perhaps a gypsy, and 'The dancer'. This is an unusual and clever song, it contains fast talking lyrics with Joni again sounding like Joan Baez. 'Penance' is the narrator warning the dancer of a sailor that will come to port and take her heart with a kiss. The 'Dancer' dances in a smoky bar frequented by sailors. 'Penance' herself has been wooed by the sailor, he once brought her silks and Persian lace. As the story unravels we learn that 'Penance' has probably murdered the sailor. The 'Dancer's' responses are almost washed away by 'Penance's' words. The 'Dancer' is waiting for him to return, 'Penance' is convinced that 'Dancer' knows the answer. A who-dunnit with not enough clues for us to solve the mystery. I thought at the time that Joni had been reading the books of Washington Irving, Joni's song definitely has the same sympathetic touch. Irving's 'Ichabod Crane' disappears in mysterious circumstances in his 'The Legend of Sleepy Hollow', additionally 'Bracebridge Hall' contains tales of pirates, buried treasure, ghost ships, all as part of romantic episodes. Of course Washington Irving was better known as the writer of the story of 'Rip Van Winkle'.

SONG TO A SEAGULL: This song should have been sequenced as the first track on side two, she is out of the city but remembering what it was like when she was there. She lived there alone like Robinson Crusoe, flowers were false, it had concrete pavements where there should have been beaches. Joni wants to re-create her seaside within the city, the ambivalence of liking both types of life style rears its ugly head, if only they could be one and the same. Of course Los Angeles, New York and San Francisco Joni's habitual haunts will all be very close to the sea, perhaps she was so restless she just could never decide.

CACTUS TREE: Written by Joni after she had seen Bob Dylan's film 'Don't Look Back'. She said that the film made a big impression on her, the song could almost be a Dylan song. In her performance Joni can be heard lengthening her A's to sound like Bob. Her heart is full and hollow just like a cactus tree. Joni once said that this song concerns a woman that had broken a thousand men's hearts. I never realised that Joni was in fact singing about the same woman throughout the song, but of course the fourth verse does indicate that fact. The first man is a schooner owner (this might be David Crosby), there is also a mountaineer, a fan who sent a letter, a soldier, a store owner, a jouster, a jester, a drummer and a dreamer and even more. This lady must be Joni, yet with all these admirers she still wishes to be free, she is busy being free. The third verse may indicate that husband Chuck Mitchell had his name on her papers, but would he be sharing her profits at the time? Is this Joni's record deal, is it her manager, is it.....? The modern woman wanted to be free, female freedom and awareness was growing, a new emancipation of woman power. Women wanted to 'have' captivating men but not be captivated themselves. The desire for marriage and being a housewife was declining, women wanted their own domestic stability without a man. Of course the best laid plans of any woman can collapse when confronted by true-love. Joni would comment on this on a later album titled 'Court and Spark'. Cactus Tree would feature years later on the 'Hejira' album but there it is transformed to be the name of a hotel somewhere in the journey.

The album received good reviews, some critics compared Joni with Laura Nyro, it is true there are similarities in song style, piano playing and voice texture. The album crept in the Billboard charts stopping at No 189.

It was November 1968, David Crosby had a new friend in Graham Nash an Englishman that had suddenly left the group The Hollies (on December 8th) when he wanted to remain in the U.S.A. after their tour. David Crosby could see that his girlfriend Joni only had eyes for Nash, he did not stand in their way. This was obviously the mark of a good friend because Crosby did not let it affect their relationship. They all went sailing together, David soon found a new lady to share his life she was Christine Hinton. For some reason Joni affectionately called Graham Nash 'Willy'. At The Miami Pop Festival in December 28th Joni participated with Fleetwood Mac, Marvin Gaye, Canned Heat and Three Dog Night. Elliot Roberts had managed to fill Joni's booking schedule on the strength of her first album, she would go on the road touring for 40 weeks. Meanwhile in London, David Crosby, Stephen Stills and Graham Nash were rehearsing new songs and preparing to record their first album.

At this time the songs 'Jeremy' and 'Winter Lady' were registered to Joni Mitchell but I have unable to locate copies or recordings of either song.

CLOUDS (1969)

He (Anthony) has a cloud on his face,
he were the worse for that, were he a horse.
William Shakespeare (Anthony and Cleopatra)

Crosby Stills and Nash can't agree on the time nor place that they first harmonised together and decided that they had a wonderful sound. It was either at Cass Elliot's house or at Joni's. Stephen Stills claims the former, Nash the latter, Crosby can't decide on either. Cass had been the matchmaker for Nash and Joni, although they initially met through Stills, who also introduced Nash to Crosby; Joni was of course David Crosby's lady at the time. Stephen Stills composed 'Judy Blue Eyes' for Judy Collins, David Crosby wrote 'Guinevere' for Joni Mitchell, both songs were included on the first C.S.N. eponymously titled album. David Crosby did not admit that 'Guinevere' was for Joni, in The C.S.N. Boxed set he states.."songs are seldom about one person, it is a love song, an answer to some other love songs, a part of a conversation". Surely the Graham Nash song 'Lady of the Island' was also for Joni, wasn't it?

Joni was touring America, she played at the music festivals at Newport, Shaefer-New York (with Tim Hardin), Big Sur, Atlanta, Montery (where she opened for Crosby Stills and Nash) and New York. The Big Sur Festival was filmed (released as 'Celebration') and shows Joni sitting on an open stage in front of a swimming pool which is adjacent to a cliff edge down to the sea. It was on February 1st 1969 that Joni that made her debut performance at New York's Carnegie Hall. This was the year of Woodstock, the flower power generation got together for some music on Yasgur's farm, not in Woodstock but many miles up the road in Bethel. Joni was booked to appear and according to The Guinness Book of Rock Stars the reason for her non appearance was... 'that David Geffen advised her not to go as she had a commitment to appear on The Dick Cavett Television Talk Show'. Joni stated that after recording The Cavett Show in the morning she made an effort to get to the airport to fly to Woodstock accompanied by David Geffen, but due to bad weather, they decided to return to Manhattan. As Joni was booked to appear on Sunday Night and record for Dick Cavett's show on Monday perhaps the whole explanation should be turned on its head? Whatever happened Joni wrote the song of the festival from the point of view of a girl who could not get to the party. Although she never appeared at Woodstock most of the non-music lay-public believe that she did. In the book included with the C.S.N. boxed set, Joni wrote that during Woodstock she was glued to the media, the exasperated kid that couldn't make it to the party. At this time Joni had become a born again christian, she had given up all religion at an early age. She said and I quote... 'Suddenly as performers we were in the position of having so many people look to us for leadership, and for some unknown reason I took it seriously and decided I needed a guide and leaned on God. So I was a little God-mad at the time. I had been saying to myself where are the modern miracles? Woodstock impressed me as if it was a modern miracle, like a modern-day fishes-and-loaves story'.

Graham Nash and Joni set up home in her house in Laurel Canyon, on Lookout Mountain. In the notes in The C.S.N. boxed set Graham explained that it was such a charming house. Joni had a collection of multi-coloured glass in the window that would catch the light like fiery gems. Graham wrote the song 'Our House' about their domesticity, a fireplace, two cats in the yard, you know the rest. Joni you may remember was impressed as a child by the coloured 'gems' in The Tales of Hoffman film.

The first C.S.N. album was released in May 1969, it went gold in October. The day the trio were advised of the million sales of the album, disaster struck. Christine Hinton, David Crosby's new partner had visited the veterinary surgeon with their pet cats. She was driving their Volkswagen Mini-Bus home when she was involved in a head-on collision and she was killed. David Crosby has never recovered from his loss; almost co-incidently Joni's second album was released.

CLOUDS (Released October 1969)

The album had another Joni Mitchell designed cover. It was a full-face portrait, yet apparently only part of a much larger painting. Joni is holding a flower in her left hand. Her blue eyes stare out at us, Joni has even included the freckles on the bridge of her nose. She is standing in front of a wooded area, to her left is what is probably a Canadian City, to her right and on the cover rear is a broad yellow and red sky and some mountains which skirt a river. The album was dedicated to Joni's maternal grandmother Sadie McKee. Unlike the first album there are no other musicians augmenting her on the album. The album was recorded at A&M Studios Hollywood, Joni did not employ a producer except for the first track 'Tin Angel' where she was assisted by Henry Lewy, although Paul Rothchild has been subsequently credited with the production of this track.

The quotation from Shakespeare's 'Anthony and Cleopatra' which heads this chapter may be vague to you. A 'cloud' is a dark spot on the forehead of a horse, between the eyes. A pale or white spot would be called a 'star'. Joni uses 'Clouds' as a dividing line between life and illusion, although other meanings are rife in the English language. For example 'under a cloud' can mean under suspicion, 'every cloud has a silver lining' is for looking on the bright side, 'head in the clouds' is for a dreamer. Of course 'cloud-cuckoo-land' is an imaginary city built in the sky by birds in a book by Aristophanes, it proves to be an impractical utopian dream. I wondered at the time if perhaps Aristophanes may have been the inspiration for the song, there is an affinity of outlooks; read The Nephelococcygia of The Birds to understand the reasons for my ambivalence.

TIN ANGEL: Is certainly influenced by the songs of David Crosby. A song for finding someone to love, someone to take a chance on. A tin angel another knight in shining armour, or an angel who has been hurt so often they have become protected or immune to the hurt and pain by a metal-like impenetrable carapace.

CHELSEA MORNING: Back in the city, living in Chelsea. The traffic noise outside, she open the curtains and lets the day in. The streets are untidy with discarded paper flying about and scavenging pigeons the only birds. The Sun's prismatic reflections of the rainbow reminds Joni of crystal beads, or jewel light. She settles down for breakfast it seems that she is now happy in the city and not homesick for the seaside. An up-tempo song which is extremely memorable, in the first verse she hears, in the second she sees, by the third she knows. This and a couple of the other songs on the album were written in 1967, recorded in 1969 but not registered to Siquomb Publishing until 1974, perhaps they were just re-assigned.

I DON'T KNOW WHERE I STAND: This track and Chelsea Morning were both recorded by Fairport Convention in the U.K. The sheet music states that she is all alone in Carolina but at the time of recording Joni had 'moved' the place in the song to California. Of course James Taylor went to 'Carolina in his Mind' on his first (and only Apple label album) album in 1970. In the song she is in the situation of so many lovers. Does she write to him, does she call, will the response be affirmative? If she doesn't know then the situation of hope remains, once she makes contact then the anticipation of love could be quenched immediately. It is probably best not to know where she stands.

THAT SONG ABOUT MIDWAY: For many years it has been assumed that this song concerns Canadian poet songwriter Leonard Cohen, he is the devil with wings playing guitar; this may be true, it may not. Joni has written an extremely poetic lyric, he stood out like a ruby in a black man's ear when she met him at Midway Fair. The protagonist was the object of the narrator's fan worship, she followed him with her satchels from town to town. This may be in the writers' imagination, it is apparent that she had tickets for his shows, yet she also infers that she saw him cheating more than once, but what at, love or gambling?

ROSES BLUE: Is a song of a gypsy girl obsessed by fortune telling, and astrology. People visit to hear her prophecy for the future, she will tell of your death but not when. One has to laugh off these doom-laden ideas, it is the only way. This song probably refers to Joni's mother Myrtle, she had her tea leaves read, a painful death forecast but no date. This theme would re-occur later in the canon of Joni Mitchell songs.

THE GALLERY: Is another song written about Leonard Cohen. Joni actually duets with herself on this track and it is a very accomplished performance. She has read about him in a magazine, he has a 'wall' of ladies, but they are his paintings? In fact she continues with the idea that he should study to portray her, the ladies' eyes on the wall follow him (her) around as he (she) moves. She has been accused of being heartless, she is cruel, but he is now with Josephine. She continues to wait keeping his house clean and repaired, she even dusts his paintings. She has been his saint in bed and given to him her pity, he is gone but might return to give her his religion. This really is a concoction of thoughts, can this really be Len Cohen, I know he writes but does he paint, or does he purchase fine art? This lyric could be a clever negative from Joni, the 'he' should be a 'she' and it is probably Joni that has the paintings and does not want the man. This is a slow song that never appears on the anthologies but the lyric is worthy of any modern poet.

I THINK I UNDERSTAND: A troubled mind, the thoughts are again out of the city. Forests and wilderlands, stepping stones and sinking sand set the scene. She is chatting to friends, listening to the church clock chime yet hoping that someone special might remember to call her back to him.

SONGS FOR AGING CHILDREN COME: The stereo mixing has separated two Joni Mitchell voices one for each speaker. The lyrics are passing images, sadness, crying, does the moon only play silver. A throbbing light machine was used in Arlo Guthrie's film 'Alice's Restaurant', the reference here seems ambiguous. The crows and ravens pick at corpses on the battle field, is this Joni hinting at the futility of the war in Vietnam? I love the use of the word 'wilder' I can't remember it being used in another song, it is a word that describes being led astray, taken from 'bewilder'. Julian Cope's Teardrop Explodes also titled an album 'Wilder', to be led astray. Perhaps Joni's 'wilderlands' are also place where children can be led to confusion and imperfection.

THE FIDDLE AND THE DRUM: Sung a-cappella this is another of Joni's songs that are full of ambivalences. The Vietnam War was certainly in her mind here, America the land of the free, not only fighting the Vietcong but fighting each other at home. I have played this a few extra times trying to work out just what Joni had in her brain at the time. She had observed students dressed in jeans being beaten with batons by the police. She realised at the time that if she had been wearing jeans she might have ben attacked too, jeans were seen by the police as the uniform of the enemy. I think that Joni was making a concerted effort to be ambiguous and political, if Bob Dylan could do it why not Joni Mitchell. Joni is asking her dear friend Tommy why he plays the fiddle and the drum, is he a policeman, she is not asking for him to be a pacifist or a deserter, she is just perplexed by his situation.

BOTH SIDES NOW: Joni has seen love from both sides, this nice and seemingly happy songs ends in pessimism and disillusionment. When she was younger clouds appeared to be ice cream castles in the sky, as she grows older and wiser they just block the sun, make it dark and pour down rain. Even her old friends look at her differently since she left home for the big city. This song has become synonymous with the name Joni Mitchell, it is the song that everyone knows. A song of childhood aspirations, a song of dreams that have changed with the passing of time. The number of artists that have recorded this song would fill a full page some of them are...Glen Campbell, Clannad, Judy Collins, Bing Crosby, Neil Diamond, Benny Goodman, George Hamilton IV, Mantovani, Anne Murray, Willie Nelson, Mary O'Hara, Frank Sinatra, Singers Unlimited, Kiri Te Kanawa, Andy Williams and Paul Young.

Assisted by many advance orders the album achieved No 31 in the charts. Joni went on The Johnny Cash Show to promote the album and it was here that she met Bob Dylan for the first time. I wonder if Johnny remembered without prompting that Joni was one of Johnny's crowned Teenage Queens?

Joni and Graham Nash spent time with David Crosby on his yacht, he needed his friends around to assist him cope with his bereavement. They took long trips in the boat whenever possible. They sailed to Jamaica then returned via The Panama Canal and up the West Coast to San Francisco where Christine Hinton's ashes were scattered adjacent to The Golden Gate Bridge. Joni joined the cruise in Jamaica but flew home from Panama. Graham was taken ill on the journey and nursed back to health by Joni, they were so happy with their lives they were certainly ascloseasthis. Graham was watching Crosby very closely worried that his depression at the loss of Christine Hinton may have given him suicidal tendencies.

Joni Mitchell

LADIES OF THE CANYON (1970)

Of things I'd rather keep in silence I must sing.
Countess of Dis (1140-?)

Joni appeared at London's Royal Festival Hall and during the performance announced that she was quitting live shows. Undoubtedly this was because of the enforced separations caused by C.S.N. and Joni touring at separate times, although this particular tour was with C.S.N. Touring together was good sense for other reasons, Elliot Roberts was manager for both Joni and C.S.N., they were both ably assisted by David Geffen who was a businessman first and a lover of music a long way behind in second place. I have always disliked these announcements of retirement, in recent years it has become an excellent form of publicity. The fans rush to see what is to be the last performance only for another retirement tour announcement a few months later; Frank Sinatra, Gary Glitter were two exponents of regular retirements.

Joni was surprised to win a Grammy Award in March, the prize was for The Best Folk Performance of 1969. Nominated and beaten by Joni were...Joan Baez 'Any Day Now', Judy Collins 'Bird on a Wire', Pete Seeger 'Young vs Old', so she had beaten off some stiff competition . Best song of the year was Joe South's 'Games People Play', Best album 'Blood Sweat and Tears' and The Best Selling Single 'Aquarius' from The Fifth Dimension. The Folk category was deleted after 1970 so folk artists had to compete in the pop music category, this was where Joni expected to be placed anyway. As she never sung traditional folk songs she considered herself a pop music performer.

LADIES OF THE CANYON (Released May 1970)

This album was destined to be Joni's first Golden Disc. It reached No 27 in the charts. Also C.S.N. had expanded to include Neil Young and become C.S.N.Y. for the recording of their 'Deja Vu' album which was released in March 1970. The single of their version of Joni's 'Woodstock' rose up the singles chart stalling at No 11. The album reached the dizzy heights of No 8 in the U.K., and Joni's single 'Big Yellow Taxi' got to number 8 in the U.K. Joni's previous album was totally solo, on this album she enlisted the help of Paul Horn, Milt Holland, Teresa Adams and Jim Horn. Joni used a play-on-words taken from her home town of Saskatoon, calling her own multi-tracked vocals as by The Saskatunes. Of course The Lookout Mountain United Downstairs Choir were in fact C.S.N.Y., although Neil Young is difficult to hear in the mix. Joni said at the time that 'her music was becoming more rhythmic due to her being in Los Angeles and that her friends were now mostly rock 'n' roll people'.

Joni's cover design was a similar layout idea to the first album a drawing that was partially coloured-in. The Mitchell handwriting used on the inner for the vinyl release disappeared when the album was released on compact disc. The cover design comprises of a sketch of Joni either holding up her dress or a sheet, perhaps a mirror. The sheet 'reflects' houses on a hill, an open garage showing the rear of a Volkswagen (probably), there is also another car some trees and plenty of grass. An artist would describe this as minimalist, a realist would describe it as unfinished. The peacocks from the first album are shown on the back but the shape of their heads probably means that they are now geese.

MORNING MORGANTOWN: Reflections of a small town, the pleasure and happiness of living there shines out from the lyrics. This could be an extension to the feelings expressed in 'Sisotowbell Lane' from the first album. There is an impish sense of humour in the life of Morgantown, the ladies are dressing up and they wink at total strangers in the street. In the last verse she is actually offering to love someone, a sexual solicitation.

FOR FREE; A song also recorded by David Crosby. The 'Diggers' of San Francisco under the leadership of Emmett Grogan were attempting to get food and clothes for the needy, for free. The flower power generation had this dream of a 'free' everything. It proved impossible when the businesses providing the free products wanted their name on them as promotional gifts, this was not the ideal of 'The Diggers' and the dream soon died. Joni prefaces this song at performances by saying that she saw a busker playing clarinet at the side of the road, for free. Joni has always changed the site of where she actually saw the busker to be within the area of her performance, when in London she said it was in The Kings Road, the area of the U.K.'s flower power masqueraders, in U.S.A. she said it was a scene from New York. Joni rhymes 'jewels' with 'schoo-els' on this excellent song where she realises that she plays for a fortune, she has things she doesn't need yet she feels that she is only as good as that busker. On the record Paul Horn plays out a clarinet solo coda representing the busker.

If you allow me to digress....I personally remember a singer songwriter playing free for me once. I was at drinking club in Tottenham, North London in the 1960's, called The Carlton Club. I must add that this was 'a' Carlton Club not

'The' Carlton Club. The club had a back room with a stage, and the front of the club, which was much larger, was a long bar. On one particular night the bar was packed with professional drinkers, I was sitting quietly reading in the back room, it was my turn for abstinence, I had to drive the drunks home. Suddenly a beautiful blonde woman entered leading a blind man who was carrying a guitar case. She left him standing alone and lost and went to get him a stool on which to sit, she placed it on the stage and led him up to the stool. He fumbled with his guitar case and microphone and then played for over an hour just to me and the blonde girl who had come to sit next to me. This busker was brilliant, he had recently appeared on Radio London, one of the offshore illegal pirate stations the week earlier, that was apparently the first live performance from one of the pirate stations. A couple of the drinkers ventured in, listened for a few moments and then returned to the bar. The young busker wearing dark glasses spoke to me (and his blonde assistant), he explained that this would be his first and last visit to the U.K. as the customs at the airport would not allow him to bring his guide dog into the country. He also, knowing there was only me listening, advised me no to clap or someone might mistake me for a seal and throw me a fish. He sang songs from his latest album, such as 'Light My Fire' and 'California Dreaming'. This so called busker two years later arrived in the U.K. and filled all his concert hall dates, he was Jose Feliciano, and he once sang for me.....for free. He was brilliant even with the knowledge that he was playing to an audience of just two people.

CONVERSATION: An exceptionally poetic lyric, the three women discussed are all Joni Mitchell. The song opens with some distinctly C.S.N.Y. acoustic guitar strumming, the song should have been titled 'Comfort and Consultation' because that is the subject of the song. Although Joni is acting as the agony-aunt she is certain that she can be a better partner for this troubled man. The man must be aware that he will find comfort from the woman. Her advice in this platonic relationship is that although he is so unhappy when they are together he feels even worse when they are apart, true of so many relationships. The song is augmented by Paul Horn's flute and Jim Horn's saxophone coda.

LADIES OF THE CANYON: 'Wampum beads' in the opening line of the lyric are cylindrical shells strung or woven together, it is shortening of the word 'wampompeag', Red Indian for 'light-string-bead'. North American Red Indians used Wampum as money. So in the song Trina is a Red Indian and a lady of the Canyon, an unlikely and unusual predicament. She is drawing and sewing, Joni does both. Anna, a mother, has little to do, so she looks after fat cats and babies. Estrella also acts like a the gypsy circus girl, but is only visiting? However when they all come together in the last verse it is evident that Estrella is Joni, playing music down the canyon and colouring. The tremolo on the last word 'canyon' in each verse is very arresting, as is the Joni Mitchell choir, or more correctly the choir of Joni Mitchells.

WILLY: A song that has been the subject of many interviews over the years. Joni admitted that it was for Graham Nash, it was his nickname anyway. Graham for the period of their arrangement had everything that Joni had searched out in a man. In the first verse she is coming to terms with his inability to give all his love due to a previous unhealed broken relationship. Joni is besotted, there have rarely been songs so personal and pleading, she wants to be her own woman but here she considers giving it all up for love. She combines sorrow together with joy. At least she managed to entwine and enchant him eventually within her spell, later when it was over this powerful all consuming love was not replaced by hate as so often happens. A song that if handled badly would have become excruciatingly embarrassing, here it is stunning. When Joni first premiered this song at the 1969 Mariposa Festival she was so filled with emotion that she had great difficulty in completing it. It became apparent later that she had written the song just as their relationship had reached its peak, it was just starting to decline.

THE ARRANGEMENT: This song is as close as Joni ever got to composing a Laura Nyro song and performance, Joni's piano playing is also similar to Laura's. This is a song of triolism, the eternal triangle where one of the three is the woman, and a wife. The apartment on the 33rd floor is probably a red-herring meant to deceive the listener when this trio may be Crosby, Nash and Mitchell, but there again.....? The song was written by Joni as the theme song for the Elia Kazan film 'The Arrangement' but it was not considered immediate enough to assist the film. The music for the film was composed by David Amran, it was the story was of a wealthy advertising man that fails in a suicide attempt and then spends his convalescence reflecting on his unsatisfactory emotional life. The reality is that Joni was told the plot outline of the film and her song was the result.

RAINY NIGHT HOUSE: This has been mooted as aimed at either Leonard Cohen or Neil Young. I suppose it could be either, I'm not sure if Leonard or Neil went out and lived in a tent in the desert. A refugee from a wealthy family out to find oneself. With James Taylor singing of his rainy day man, he would need a rainy night house to go to, perhaps.

THE PRIEST: More Leonard Cohen influences, he wrote a song titled 'Priests' which Judy Collins included on her 'Wildflowers' album, an album that also includes Joni's songs 'Both Sides Now' and 'Michael from the Mountains'. Leonard's version of the song did not appear on his own records but was only included in his music books. Leonard's song is certainly for a woman, but who? Leonard is stating that he will be her Lord and they will wear away her 'little window', whatever or wherever that is. He also knows he will be the Lord of memory, and states that she has 'red and golden paints'. He also reminds the woman in the song that he has been observed watching her when all her minds were 'Free'. Judy, Janis or Joni, which of these three 'Js' is it?

In Joni's song we are presented with 'his' contradictions. She is saying goodbye to him at an airport bar. He wanted truth and time, she wanted 'now'. The parting is emotional his eyes were asking for her, hers were ready to try, his home was neglected and run-down, they parted hoping that their love would pass in absence and not grow. A powerful lyric, Leonard's 'Priests' has similar arguments and contradictions.

BLUE BOY: Tim Hardin's song 'Lady Came from Baltimore' imposes some influence on this song. This is one of Joni's most sensual songs. There is little abstruseness here as she adds her sexual oohs and aahs. This is for old stone face, no surely it can't be Leonard Cohen again. The blue boy in the title is unlikely to be Thomas Gainsborough's 'Blue Boy', however it could be someone who always seems depressed (back to Leonard Cohen again), or a man with blue eyes, the paintings of Cohen show him with grey eyes. Joni actually writes that it was difficult to waken his face, he would give her his seed, he comes a few times more, in her 'door', wherever that is; on a previous track it was her 'little window'. The lyric sheet is necessary for the nuance of one word, Joni looks out of her window through the 'pain' not the 'pane'.

BIG YELLOW TAXI: Joni got the germ of an idea for this song when she was in Hawaii. When she awoke in the morning she looked out from her window over the beautiful landscape, but as her eyes lowered she noticed that below her was huge paved parking lot. This song she described to Ray Coleman as being 'Ecology rock 'n' roll'. In the B.B.C. 'In Concert' performance in October 1970 Joni introduced this song enthusiastically saying that Bob Dylan had written his own verse for it. In fact we would not hear Bob's version until CBS released the infamous 'Dylan' album in 1973, Dylan had just moved his allegiance to David Geffen's Label, the album was the

CBS response to Bob's changing affiliation. Bob's version of 'Big Yellow Taxi' changes one line where he replaces the taxi for 'A big yellow bulldozer' which 'took away my house and land'. Let us hope that they have not yet actually paved all of paradise. This song and 'Both Sides Now' are the songs known to peripheral music listeners as Joni's most famous, they remain her two most easily memorable songs, even the giggle at the end of the song is perfect.

WOODSTOCK: This song with all its happiness and anticipation must be juxtaposed alongside the student shootings at Kent State University and the stabbing at The Altamont Festival. As we know Joni never made it to Woodstock but everyone thinks she did, her song is the nostalgic anthem of that festival of love and music. The Ian Matthews version to my mind is the definitive, he added so much to the melody and it was deservedly a million seller. It is a shame the youth of today, as we approach the millennium, seem unable to 'get back to the garden', and I don't mean horticulture.

THE CIRCLE GAME: Although this has C.S.N.Y. backing I can't hear Neil Young. This is the song of life and how it all comes full circle, the Byrds sang of this in 1973. The song was written for Neil Young, although it is also Joni reminiscing of her days in Saskatchewan. From birth in the first verse, ages 10,16 and 20 follow, they share their dreams for the future. Joni and Neil Young (he is two years younger) of course both were struck down by polio and survived so they have this natural affinity, and also the mutual 'scorpio rising' understanding of survival and perseverance. Joni said at her Festival Hall Show that this song was written for a Canadian singer songwriter who became very sad when he reached the age of 21. He suddenly found that he was refused entrance to his favourite teenager club because he had ceased to be a teenager. He wrote 'Oh to Live on Sugar Mountain' to register his disapproval of growing so old and giving him the feeling that his life was over. Joni wrote this song for reassurance to him that 'life goes on after 21', hence the ages ending at 20 in the verses.

The title 'The Circle Game' track was not original, it was the title of a book by Canadian writer Margaret Eleanor Atwood. Atwood was born in 1939 and had lived in the Quebec bush for many years before settling in Toronto. Her book 'The Circle Game' was written in 1966 and won The General's Medal in Canada, an honour which Joni would win later in her career. Atwood's book was a collection of poems, the 'Game' was the relationships between male and female rather than the full circle of life. She also wrote that 'photographers attempt to freeze reality with their glass eye'. Joni would try to freeze moments with collage photographs on some of her later album covers. The cover of Margaret Atwood's book depicted a spiral maze not a circle, the climax of a relationship being the centre of that maze, the return trip out of the maze presented the situation of growing farther apart as time passes. Margaret Atwood also won another General's prize in 1985 for her book 'The Handmaid's Tale'.

The critics reaction to Joni's album was once again, mixed. Nick Kent recognised as the top U.K. writer at the time went over the top with his brand new thesaurus, his rhetoric totally missing the point. He accused her of presenting 'the fey paraphernalia of the whole loathsome Laurel Canyon tradition'. Paul Gambaccini thought the whole album poetic. The Rolling Stone Magazine when listing special albums of the past five years in 1974 wrote of the album...'Joni Mitchell was never the frail hippy dippy singer her appearance may have suggested, the waif-like exterior and goofy look masked not only a genuinely talented musician and writer, but someone who quickly understood the politics of pop'. But the magazine could not leave it at that they had to add 'Through the summer of love era Mitchell furthered her career by romancing most of C.S.N.& Y. and several Eagles, thrusting herself and her songs into the spotlight'. The Rolling Stone Magazine for some reason known only to themselves would continue to pour scorn on Joni's un-private love life, and on many occasions forgot that they were really reviewing her music; they inflicted unnecessary pain by their inconsideration.

Although Joni had decided to quit live performance she did appear at The Mariposa Festival during the summer and The Isle of Wight Festival in August. Joni appeared on the fourth day on The Isle Of Wight and was heckled from the audience, she stopped playing half way through 'Chelsea Morning'. She cleverly informed the audience that they were not treating the performers with respect, the people were acting like tourists. This seemed to embarrass the crowd into some form of good conduct and she played on, although the anger and nerves can be heard in her voice. Joni then switched to piano to sing 'Woodstock'. Brian Hinton who has chronicled the I.O.W. Festivals stated that the man that came onto the stage sat at Joni's feet and played bongo was in fact one Yogi Joe, on the recording Joni can be heard saying "This is entirely inappropriate Joe", so she obviously knew him previously. Elliot Roberts and Ian Samwell came onto the stage to evict Yogi Joe. After Joni finishes singing Yogi Joe grabbed the microphone and started shouting at the free-loaders on Desolation Hill until he was hauled away. Joni also sang For Free, Willy, Big Yellow Taxi, Both Sides Now, and two new songs 'California' and 'Good Samaritan'. Joni managed to get through the performance when so many others would have walked off the stage. Joni explained how she felt in a 'Q' Magazine interview in 1988. She said that she had been to a Hopi snake dance ceremony (she also mentioned this on stage at the festival), a rain dance. At Hopi ceremony there were charmed snakes in the ritual but one snake hurled itself into the audience scattering them in panic. What Joni remembered was that the musicians involved in the ceremony never missed a beat, they never flinched from the snake, the importance of bringing the rain to the crops was far more important than avoiding a snake bite. This made Joni more resilient and determined to stay on stage and face the arrogant rudeness of the I.O.W. imbeciles. Listening to the compact disc of the event one can hear Kris Kristofferson saying during his performance, of the unsatisfactory situation, that perhaps they might even get shot. Kris says " We intend to do two more songs despite anything except rifle-fire".

Joni sang back-up vocals for James Taylor's album 'Mud Slide Slim', (released 1971) she can be heard clearly on 'You've Got A Friend', 'Love as Brought Me Around' and 'Long Ago and Far Away'. Joni also helped out Carole King on 'Tapestry' which would be a multi-million selling album. This meeting with James Taylor would herald the conclusion of the relationship with Graham Nash. Joni appeared on two versions of 'You've Got a Friend' a song written by Carole King.

As Joni seemed to be moving quickly from one lover to another, The Rolling Stone Magazine titled Joni rather cruelly 'Queen of El Lay' and 'Old Lady of the Year'. This is more hurtful and sexist when one considers Jim Morrison writing a lyric titled 'Back Door Man' concerning anal sex which brought almost no comment or criticism from the music press. Changing relationships continued to be perfectly alright for men but not for women, there were plenty of promiscuous men, as usual all presented as 'exciting-young-men'. There was also a family tree created depicting Joni's many alleged relationships, these included Crosby, Nash, Stills, Young, Russ Kunkel, Leonard Cohen, Warren Beatty, Jackson Browne, and even David Geffen of whom it was later alleged was in fact homosexual.

Joni was preparing to marry Graham Nash when she suddenly terminated the relationship in favour of new beau James Taylor. They parted on the day before C.S.N. performance at Fillmore East in June. Graham Nash continues the story ..."I broke up with Joni Mitchell and my whole world fell apart. The afternoon of that Fillmore East Show I wrote the song 'Simple Man' and in the evening I performed it live for the first time, with Joni sitting in the audience - I don't know how I got through that". Graham recalls this in his notes in the C.S.N. boxed set. Of course Graham also composed 'I Used to Be a King' which is his answer-back record to Joni's 'I Had a King' which was written about former husband Chuck Mitchell. Graham said that his song was another 'King Midas in Reverse' (a hit for the Hollies), recalling the King he once was.

The Melody Maker music paper readers poll voted Joni Mitchell top female singer. In September back in England Joni recorded a television special for the B.B.C. where she sang even though she was suffering with a bad cold. In October, Matthews Southern Comfort led by Ian Matthews took the more melodic and smooth version of Joni's 'Woodstock' to the top of the U.K. charts; it also did very well in the U.S.A. reaching No 23 in April of 1971

At her Royal Festival Hall Concerts at the end of November Joni seemed more vulnerable than ever. It was as if the power of thought from the audience was willing her to carry on through adversity. She was forgetting the words of songs, also finding that she just could not tune her guitar properly. At least she managed to remain on friendly terms with Graham Nash as on that night he and manager Elliot Roberts came on stage to act as backing vocalists. Joni appeared in Concert at The Royal 'Albert' Hall with James Taylor. There seems to be great deal of confusion over the actual venue of the show. This is exacerbated by the bootleg recordings. The 'Live at The BBC 1970' and 'Live at The Royal Albert Hall 1970' albums are the same performances. I have one collection with extra tracks by James Taylor but the-between-song banter is identical. It is my opinion that the recordings are from The BBC Shows (September 1970), the audience does not have the ambience of either Festival or Albert Hall.

She seemed extremely happy at the time although she was gradually losing her voice as the show progressed. I purchased one copy of the album of the show in a sale in major high street record shop, they and I, had no idea at the time that it was in fact a bootleg. The recording is superb, the engineering is so good that the album deserved a full release. Joni sang 'Gallery' explaining that it was written for a connoisseur who toured the world collecting 'beauties', and then connoisseuring them. James is his usually laid back self especially on 'Steamroller' where he incited himself to new heights of pedestrian guitaring in the solo break, all lazily performed to the audience's great delight. Joni sings 'The Priest' with no introduction, but before she sings 'Carey' she informs us that it concerns a friend from 'everywhere', at the show she was smiling at Taylor making it pretty obvious that it was aimed at him, she does her giggle at the end as if she has just been dared by James to sing something extremely naughty.

Joni then gives us a lecture on the Appalachian dulcimer that she was playing. She indicates that the tuning is 'Matala' tuning, she had lived at Matala for five weeks in rural surroundings. She was living in caves cut into the hillsides by the early Greeks and Romans, it was there that she met Yogi Joe who interrupted her performance at The Isle of Wight Festival. After James sings 'Carolina in My Mind' they sing Joni's 'California' although James has problems getting the opening correct. 'For Free' is introduced as Joni's 'Happy Trails to You', Joni turns to James and says "I'm ready when you are", he responds with "I know". After 'The Circle Game' the album is completed by Taylor's beautiful lullaby 'You Can Close Your Eyes', in my opinion one of his greatest compositions. Just before they commence singing Joni laughs and hums the theme of 'I'll Get By With a Little Help from my Friends'. Of course the album was not the complete show but perhaps it should be released officially now.

Joni was also becoming more itinerant in the style of Jack Kerouac's 'On the Road' the wanderlusting travellers bible. She had particularly loved Matala in Greece, and of course fellow Canadian Leonard Cohen was also becoming a lover of Greek Islands. This idyllic rural lifestyle can be enjoyed more when it is undertaken in the knowledge that it can be escaped just as soon as one tires of it.

BLUE (1971)

He who sings scares away his woes
Miguel de Cervantes (1547-1616)

Joni took some time off, the pain of the ending of her relationship with Graham Nash and coming to terms with James Taylor's demanding personality took their toll on her emotions. She was writing increasingly introverted songs, trying, as Stephen Stills said, 'to exorcise her demons and ghosts' in her lyrics. This remark brings the words 'kettle' and 'black' to mind in a sentence, one only has to listen to Still's excruciatingly beautiful 'To A Flame' from his first solo album to see that he would eventually do exactly the same. Joni's next album 'Blue' would be more heart-rending and emotional than ever. Joni could not complete the song 'Willy' at The Mariposa Festival, and at The I.O.W. Festival she cried, then she sat in silence and became very angry with the audience. These were extremely trying times for Joni but she had a greater resilience than her gentle countenance portrayed. This was Joni Mitchell the girl with her head in the 'Clouds' who could see 'Both Sides Now', the little girl had grown up, and fast.

Graham Nash recorded his first solo album 'SONGS FOR BEGINNERS' (released 1971) which was released on Atlantic. The album is littered with songs for Joni. 'Better Days', in which Graham states that she has moved away chasing mirrors through a haze. 'Wounded Bird' has Graham talking to himself, facing the pain, trying to understand why she has left him, he is trying to swallow humble pie. 'I Used to Be a King' is a direct answer-back to Joni's 'I Had a King' although that song was for Chuck Mitchell. It seems that all Joni's lovers were, in her eyes, 'Kings'.

The Hollies also sang 'King Midas in Reverse', the similarities in the sentiments of this song are similar. When they were together everything turned to gold, now he is left without a hand to hold. The album also includes the heartbreaking 'Simple Man' written at the time of the break-up. 'Man in the Mirror' (with a false start) concerns his lack of self confidence, and surely 'Sleep Song' is as tender a love song as Graham has ever written. When Roy Carr wrote his review for the Melody Maker he compared all the songs with the work of John Lennon and said it was far from the CSNY format, I wonder if he still thinks the same? Roy Carr wrote in his review 'Graham Nash has come to terms with his life, the majority of the material pivots around love-lost and found, past present and perhaps future - Nash doesn't wallow in self pity, pathos or hide under the doom clouds of despair'. One wonders if Roy

Carr ever listened to the album. I personally felt that Joni was still singing in a style very close to that of Laura Nyro, both singers were living their lives through their songs. Nyro's voice was somewhat more shrill but the song themes were similar, most of them filled with the sentiments of love and loss. Both Laura and Joni seemed to be hoping for a knight in shining armour to come along and make their life complete.

The Hollies had a dig at Graham Nash for leaving them by releasing their own song 'Hey Willy', even the B-side was saying something to Graham in the title 'Row the Boat Together'. David Crosby had suffered as being replaced by a horse on The Notorious Byrd Brothers sleeve, so they now had something else in common.

Joni decided that it was time to go back on tour and travelled across America and Europe with Jackson Browne; Jackson (and Joni) had a song 'Shadow Dream Song' included on 'The Circle Game' album by Tom Rush. Jackson had been signed by David Geffen when he was seen at a performance at Echo Park. At the same time David Geffen saw 'Longbranch Penny Whistle' signed them and changed their name to The Eagles. The Eagles then recorded Jackson Browne's 'Take It Easy' and started their journey to international M.O.R. super-stardom. Jackson and Joni played to packed houses, but it was 1972 before Jackson Browne's first album 'Saturate Before Using' was released. Strangely, as with Joni Mitchell's first album it was also known just as 'Jackson Browne' because people didn't know where to read the title.

Joni was at last in the Top 40 in the Billboard Charts although only as a backing singer. The track 'You've Got A Friend' that she had recorded with James Taylor shot to No 1 in the charts. The follow-up single 'Long Ago and far Away' almost went top 30 stalling at No 31, the acknowledgement that it was James and Joni was more pronounced with this second single.

BLUE (released July 1971)

The first album cover from Joni not to include one of her paintings. The album cover is a blue and white photograph. Joni fills the cover with her saddened face, I have always wondered if the five splashes at the lower part of the portrait are tears, they seem to be bouncing off her bottom lip. The early releases were printed on a dark blue textured card with the lyrics on the inside of the gatefold. This is an album of songs written when Joni was at her most fragile. It was said at the time that this album bared her soul and that of James Taylor, he is certainly the recipient object of many of the songs.

On the album Joni was augmented by Stephen Stills (bass), James Taylor (guitar), 'Sneaky' Pete Kleinow (pedal steel guitar) and Russ Kunkel (drums). The dictionary terminology for 'BLUE' of course is a title for numerous blue winged butterflies and also subjects deemed to be indecent titillating and pornographic; 'BLUES' is also depressed, moody, sad and unhappy. 'BLUE' in the past tense is spending extravagantly and wastefully. In Australia 'BLUE' is a name given to a man with 'red hair', so you can now take your pick. In this album Joni has taken her now expected autobiographical songs and made them more personal and explicit. For this album she has predominantly drawn on her most recent experiences.

ALL I WANT: The aspirations of looking for love and only finding pain. This song is full of the anticipation and hopes for love. Joni' lists her fantasies, she wants to shampoo him, kiss him, renew him. Joni has juxtaposed the loneliness and travelling, in fact she is talking of life's journey. Her difficult relationship with James Taylor was the catalyst for may of the songs, she found him intolerably spoilt and demanding, but of course that was the attraction. So many women are drawn to men that are usually describes as 'rats', the inconsideration is like a magnet to beautiful women who are accustomed to reliable men who do their bidding slavishly. James Taylor is playing one of the guitars on this track, is it really Joni on the other? If this opening song is full of the joy, then the jealousy greed and the killing of happiness follows later.

MY OLD MAN: Happy with Graham Nash, in love, together without the necessity to be married. If Joni was in perfect harmony with Graham, or comfortable is a better explanation, then many women will consider her a fool to change it all for the undependable James Taylor. Joni uses some excellent metaphors in this lyric, Nash is the 'warmest chord she has ever heard', and the lines which state that the bed is too big and the frying pan's too wide may be her best lines ever, they perfectly explain the sudden change from togetherness to being alone. The remark would also aptly apply to any woman who has had a bereavement, a sublime Joni Mitchell lyric.

LITTLE GREEN: The oldest song on the album, it was registered in 1967. This is a song for Joni's adopted daughter Kelly. This is another of Joni's extremely personal songs, the listener has the feeling that they should not be listening to a woman telling all. At the time few of the fans would be aware that Joni had a daughter that she had given up. In the second verse Joni changes the gender, although she might be referring to the father of the child who is a non-conformist. At least in her imagination she was receiving poems and updates on her well being. The hopes of a mother for a child she might never see again, a child who will never know her real mother, such sadness and pain.

CAREY: Some women will forgive their men everything, especially for love. 'Carey' comes well within that category, women will give up anything for that 'Mr Right' when he comes along, here Joni is suffering from insomnia, has filthy fingernails, feet covered in tar, sleeping rough and not smelling good, and all in the first verse. The suggestion is that men go out and get drunk, she doesn't like living in this town, but she stays because he is there. I expect that James Taylor was content being called a 'mean old dog', but is he also 'the bright red devil?' Taylor later released an album titled 'One Man Dog'.

BLUE: I have always assumed that this song was for David Crosby but many writers consider this another song for James Taylor. Lost at sea in a boat or just lost? The ink of a pin is a tattoo with an empty space to fill in, but Joni's list leaves nothing to the imagination, acid, grass, needles and booze. Through all this adolescent hedonism Joni still loves him but she intends to think long and hard about the next step, 'she is gonna take a look around it'.

CALIFORNIA: James Taylor wrote a song of homesickness with 'I'm Going to Carolina in My Mind', now it is Joni's turn. The 'red devil' from 'Carey' returns this time on a Grecian Island, he stole her camera and sold it. This reads like a letter sent to Graham Nash explaining her situation, strung out on another man, take me as I am. The Grecian Island may of course mean meeting old friend Leonard Cohen again, it could be a permutation of many. James Taylor adds guitar and Sneeky Pete Kleinow is on pedal steel guitar on what is another 'blue' masterpiece. A predominant sadness of Graham Nash was that his father purchased a stolen camera from a workmate and was subsequently sent to jail. It broke the health of his father who had no idea that the camera was stolen, I wondered if Joni's reference to a stolen camera may be in remembrance of that unhappy fact.

THIS FLIGHT TONIGHT: The tune is very similar to 'Carey'. The song is for Joni flying away after ending the relationship and then having second thoughts during the flight. The nuance of the in-flight headphones playing 'Goodbye Baby Love is Blind' is a curious twist, by the time she lands she is worrying over him like a mother, have you remembered to turn the heat on, have you fixed your car.

RIVER: A sad song of lost love and the subsequent loneliness of Christmas. The song opens with 'Jingle Bells' to set the scene. We are left wondering if 'Green' is her daughter again, is 'baby' her man or 'Kelly'. One thing that is certain is that she is sad to be alone at Christmas. Back home in Saskatchewan she would be skating on the rivers at Christmas; 'Jingle Bells' is played in a minor key as if to confirm that sadness. The man concerned in the song made her weak in the knees with his sexual naughtiness. She also realises that she has been selfish and lost him, it is likely that her selfishness was in fact her possessiveness, which in an all-consuming love relationship the woman is more likely to be monogamous than the man. The sentiments of the song are extremely close to self pity. At least she consoles herself by asserting that she intends to make a lot of money and then get out of the music business.

A CASE OF YOU: The 'devil' is mentioned twice in this song, this makes for a total of four times on one album. It has been mooted that this song is for either James Taylor or Leonard Cohen. Joni refers to Canada in the first verse and that they both came from there, so that would make the protagonist Cohen. The advice from another woman was that he was difficult, this transfers the principal object of the song back to Taylor. Joni mentioned in an interview that she found the relationship with Taylor difficult predominately because of his temperament. What I don't understand from Joni's lyrics is that she is obviously in love with whoever is the object of the song, but she could 'drink' a 'case of him' without being knocked over, strange that, low potency perhaps. My impression is that it is all one-sided, her love is strong his love-power towards her is weak, she can not get enough of him, or perhaps he just doesn't give enough of himself. The verses detail the set-backs in the romance, yet by the time each chorus unfolds she re-affirming her love and addiction to him.

THE LAST TIME I SAW RICHARD: Another song for ex-husband Chuck Mitchell, Richard in the song accuses Joni of useless romanticism. It is him that stays up watching television whilst she is upstairs waiting for him to come to bed, she needed someone to help her fly away from the humdrum drudgery of their existence together. When love failed they turned to drink, or he did. I love the line 'you got tombs in your eyes', he had no ambition yet his songs were full of dreams. Joni decides in the final two lines of the album to fly away, the cafe lifestyle (where she was playing and singing) was just a phase, everything is upwards from here. At least it closes this melancholy album with some aspirations.

Timothy Crouse in his review of the album for Rolling Stone Magazine said that on this album referring to Joni 'her love has become a religious quest, and surrendering to loneliness is a sin'. Tim Crouse continued 'It is only a short step from that to Joni's vow that she will walk through hell-fire for her man. Joni has created an album from her domestic upheavals, Bob Dylan did the same with his 'Blood on the Tracks' album. During her interview with Cameron Crowe Joni said that there was 'hardly a dishonest word or note' on the album, she had torn her ego to shreds, dispelling all of her ghosts simultaneously. Perhaps in her youth she was a girl who just could not keep a secret, or alternatively wanted everything out in the open rather than simmering below the surface. Many writers over the years choose to disarm critics by self denigration, or complete honesty, it extinguished the attacks at first base.

The album should have closed with the track 'Blue' rather than place it at the end of the first side, it says everything she had in her heart at the time. The listener approaching the album for the first time would expect it to be dismal and dreary, it is not. It is packed full of wonderful songs and profound lyrics, an album as powerful now as when it was first released, all new listeners should start with 'Blue'.

The album reached No 3 in U.K. and 15 in U.S.A., a single 'Carey' extracted from the album spent just one week in the U.S. Hot 100 Charts at No 93. Joni decided yet again to take a break from the business and moved to a retreat in Vancouver where she could get back to nature and have some time to think. Understandably with the terrible attention that the music press had aimed at her many love entanglements, she needed some time out of the public glare.

FOR THE ROSES (1972)

Do not commit your poems to pages alone.
Sing them I pray you.
                    Virgil (70-19BC)

Elliot Roberts Joni's manager decided that she should change labels to Asylum Records. This was for an uncomplicated reason, it was not to boost sales but because it was alleged that David Geffen and Elliot Roberts were in fact 'an item'. Joni became, like most artists, restless with her new quiet lifestyle in Vancouver and decided to tour Europe once again. Although the music reference books state that she took a one year sabbatical, Brian Hinton in his book 'Both Sides Now' states that it was in fact two years that Joni took off. Joni was touring with Jackson Browne in July 1971 and she was again on the road in Europe in early May 1972. In England Joni also recorded for 'The Sounds For Saturday Show' which was broadcast in June.

FOR THE ROSES (Released December 1972)

The cover was a specially designed gatefold with an extra flap, an expensive layout, I had never seen one of similar design previously. The cover's coloured photograph shows Joni her hair bleached by the sun-and-sea she appears more blonde than ever. She is dressed in deep green velvet (or velour) and is wearing a pair of knee high leather boots. She is looking at the cameraman (Joel Bernstein) pensively. She is sitting close to the edge of a cliff with a wooded area behind her, there are leaves on the ground so it may have been taken in early autumn. The lyrics are to the left of the first gatefold, to the right on an extra flap is a watercolour painting of flowers and foliage by Joni, are they supposed to be roses to present the album's title? More lyrics on the next page and a nude photograph of Joni standing on some rocks looking out across an expanse of blue water towards some islands. If Joni's house was on the coast of Vancouver then she would be looking towards Vancouver Island across the Juan de Fuca Strait, it certainly looks placid and beautiful.

The original title for this album was to be taken from the last track 'Judgement of the Moon and Stars'. The nude picture of Joni was to be made into a collage that appeared to imitate a Magritte painting. Joni changed her mind when Elliot Roberts pointed out that the shop keepers would gleefully stick the price tag on her bare bottom. Joel Bernstein who also took this photograph was running the gauntlet of being incorporated as another of Joni's 'relationships', she certainly felt at ease with him seeing her naked, but as she looked so good naked she most likely was very happy to have her body-shape photographed for posterity. I am a little sceptical that the nude photograph would, with the changes anticipated, have appeared similar to a Rene Magritte painting.

Rene Magritte died in 1967, it must be said that he has been over-looked by many art historians, so many art books just miss him out completely. He is often compared to Salvador Dali and the style was similar, but the subject matter used by Magritte was not expressing his fantasies, as was Dali's. Magritte painted what are termed 'real landscapes' through a window, and later in 1994 Joni would add some of her 'real landscapes' to the compact disc booklet for 'Turbulent Indigo'. My own personal feeling towards the nude photograph is that Joni's stance on the rock is representing an almost perfect view as if taken from the rear of Botticelli's 'Birth of Venus', but it may be just a coincidence. Botticelli's Venus stands on an open sea-shell, Joni the modern day representation stands on a rock in the sea.

The title of the album is a Joni Mitchell witticism, she wanted the cover to be a photograph of a horse's arse. This premise was proved by her design of an advert used to publicise the album in Billboard, the top U.S.A. music trade paper, remember it is horse-manure that goes on the 'Roses'. The advert design depicted a toy horse's head, a bubble, surrounded by lips, an eye, a limousine, a whale and a tree in blossom, the composition meant to form Joni's features. I wondered if it was a toy horse because 'toy horse manure' is extremely rare.

On the 'Roses' album are Tommy Scott (woodwind/reeds), Wilton Felder (bass), Russ Kunkel (drums), Bobbye Hall (percussion), Graham Nash (harmonica), James Burton (electric guitar) and Stephen Stills (a rock 'n' roll band?), they all augmented at some stage. Joni also includes James Burton better known for his work on Elvis Presley records and Graham Nash reverting to harmonica used so many times in his Hollies days; Bobby Notkoff a violinist is noted as adding 'strings'.

BANQUET: The first verse is quite straight-forward, a banquet with too much to eat, people eating from a table laden high with food increasing the size of their bellies. As a digression Joni herself has hardly put on a pound weight she started out, she is in wonderful shape on the cover picture. The second verse tackles the American dream and the many choices and directions. Heroin, Jesus, a family, business deals and lazing around. Joni has returned from the city life to the sea, painting and relaxing. Just when Joni has lured us into her false sense of security she hits us below the belt. The last verse is a message to the greedy from the needy. Some people get gristle and marrow-bone, some even get the 'gravy', whilst others get nothing. A catalogue of the excesses available to the rich and famous, trying to make some sense of their lazy self indulgent lifestyle.

COLD BLUE STEEL AND SWEET FIRE: The sounds of paranoia of living in the city. Joni segues the lyric to form a stream of consciousness style, it is as if one thought collides with another and takes the song off at a tangent. Seclusion underground, she goes down the ladder. It seems that Lady Release is heroin or some other drug, paying for it with stolen goods or her own wristwatch or ring. Blood mixed with filthy water, the cold blue steel needle awaits in this city, 'a concrete concentration camp'. The song describes graphically the helplessness of the addict, you are going to take it sooner or later. All this neglect is sung to some superb harmonies, the stereo separation is particularly arresting on this track. James Burton's electric guitar playing here is just perfect.

BARANGRILL: This is for the people who work in mundane jobs but make the best of the situation. The waitresses, the truck driver and the petrol-pump attendant. They all have ways of making their jobs more pleasant, the garage worker sings songs for the customers making up his own words and tune as he goes. The waitress is hoping for a tip and thinking of her boy friend, the truck driver wants to eat and ogles the waitress hopefully. Joni is observing that they are trapped, she escaped from her salesgirl lifestyle, but it was a means to an end, that job was as important to her career as any, at the time. Tommy Scott adds some excellent flute to the backing. This song examines the situation of the indigent, the exorbitance of the wealthy was scrutinised in the earlier 'Banquet'.

LESSON IN SURVIVAL: Joni moves to piano for this song. The lyric is so personal one wonders if we should be listening to it. The lyric is self-centred, almost egotistical, the feeling it presents is that 'it was not my fault'. Joni seemed to be ending so many relationships she certainly knew about self-survival, especially for an incurable and sensitive romantic. She decides to leave, she needs time alone, she makes plans on how she will handle the situation. As soon as he enters the room she buckles and re-states her love for him, is it Nash the friend and lover or Taylor the impossible man, or...?; the song segues into...
....LET THE WIND CARRY ME: A song for Bill and Myrtle, Joni's parents. Mother provides the discipline and warns against the perils of growing up too

early. Just like all mothers she is caring and advising, and just like all children this is misconstrued as interference. Father is intervening on his daughter's behalf, even with the mother's control she still considers that she has spoilt the child. It seems that Joni (if it is Joni in the song) gets broody for a child of her own and a settled family life but it passes.

FOR THE ROSES: Another long lyric of loneliness and the thoughts that follow. Joni is thinking of James Taylor and his guitar playing and singing, and his subsequent success. She doesn't see him any more except on television, she is warning him that he is being built up to be knocked down, in fact Joni thinks that they will crucify him. She sits alone listening to the wind through the trees, it sounds just like applause.

SEE YOU SOMETIME: Is this a sequenced continuation from the previous track? It may not be James Taylor again, it may be David Geffen. This song is a self-reassurance that she has recovered from her broken heart. Although the song lyric preaches confidence and recovery Joni sings the song in a sad and pessimistic voice. Joni invites him to see her, she knows he has fame and fortune but she advises that she is not ready to marry him. They started out so kind towards each other and it ended heartlessly.

ELECTRICITY: The idea for the song may have been an electrical blackout, a fuse or power failure. Joni uses this as a metaphor for damaged love that requires repair. It is freezing, the fuses blow, two women with a technical manual repair the problem by lamp-light by trial and error. In the loving relationship the lines over-loaded, sparks, friction, now all they need is a manual so they can fix the romance. The last line of the song is the resignation that it can't be fixed. The backing on this song sounds just like C.S.N.Y. but seems to be just a choir of many Joni Mitchells.

YOU TURN ME ON I'M A RADIO: Graham Nash playing his Hollies style blues harmonica. Joni again talking to an estranged lover. He has to listen to her on the radio, she hopes that she still turns-him-on. The protagonist in question does not like weak or strong willed women, which leaves him with little choice. I love the way Joni slurs the words 'dirty' and 'Breakfast'.
Joni uses the word 'feral' which means savage, brutal, living in a wild uncultivated state. I thought she was in Vancouver to relax and re-charge her mental batteries?

BLONDE IN THE BLEACHERS: For the un-initiated 'bleachers' are a tier of seats in a sports stadium, they are sited in the inexpensive unroofed area.

A rock 'n' roll song on which it is alleged that Joni is referring to James Taylor leaving with a groupie who was sitting in the bleachers. Joni as a girl on the stage realises that there are more female groupies than male. The relationship with the groupie will not last very long, just a passing phase.

WOMAN OF HEART AND MIND: The expletive has been deleted from the lyric sheet, the white Tipp-ex and the added dots make it quite obvious on the cover that the change was made after the art work was completed, so it is a mess. The sentiments of the song are the need for some grown men to be mothered like a lost child. The person that is the object of this song is going to great lengths to impress her, she is only impressed when he is not trying. He has found God, he is imitating others, becoming a fraud. At the time it was reported that she was singing to Jackson Browne, it could be a permutation of many others. Minnie Ripperton recorded a superb version of this song on her eponymously titled album, it also was included in Minnie's 'Best Of' collection.

JUDGEMENT OF THE MOON AND STARS (Ludwig's Tune): A departure for Joni, writing a song for Ludwig Van Beethoven. The handsome Beethoven had his share of women, classical groupies perhaps. But his increasing deafness meant that he was unable to hear his music properly, yet the gift of his music continues for those who can hear. The last verse strikes off obliquely calling for passion and becomes very esoteric. Joni writes 'you have to shake your fists at lightning', she is calling for us to save the forests and the elephants. I have never been sure just what this last verse's connection had with Beethoven, but Joni sneaks in a pun saying to Beethoven 'If you're tired of 'the Silent Night', or is that just my interpretation?

The single release to promote the album was a strange choice. The song 'You Turn Me On I'm A Radio' was not taken from the album it is an alternative live recording. The B-side was also Joni's live version of 'Urge For Going' a song which up to this release was not available on any of her official albums. The choice of Asylum Records proved promotionally fortunate because it gave Joni her first top 30 hit. It entered the charts on 30th December 1972 stayed for eight weeks and reached No 25. Asylum would repeat this 'Live' release tactic in 1975 with an almost identical reaction from the public, but curiously this was for a re-release of 'Big Yellow Taxi'. Joni appeared at The Troubadour, Los Angeles for a four night sell-out season. She played for more than two hours at each show, she was so relaxed that she was conversing with the audience and prefacing many of the songs with reasons for the songs.

COURT AND SPARK (1974)

Thus it came to pass...
Jazz multiplied all over the face of the Earth,
and the wiggling of bottoms was tremendous.
                                    Peter Gammond (1925-)

Joni was now a major selling artist. 'For the Roses' moved up to reach No 11 in the Billboard Charts in February 1973. Her music publishing company was now worth $millions. With James Taylor now out of her love life, though probably not out of her thoughts, she had found a new romance with drummer John Guerin a member of Tom Scott's L.A.Express. The British group Nazareth recorded their version of Joni's 'In Flight Tonight' and it was a hit in the U.K. charts, rising to No 11. As Joni's live version 'You Turn Me On' had gone into the top 30 it was a disappointment when 'Raised on Robbery' the follow-up single could only get to No 65.

Graham Nash released another solo album titled 'WILD TALES'. Joni sung an additional vocal on a track titled 'Another Sleep Song', to be fair it is impossible to hear her, it may be her warbling away at the coda, her appearance hardly warrants a mention. Joni painted a portrait of Graham which is used for the rear of the cover. Graham is crouching, hugging his legs, he is wearing his best multi-coloured trousers. The title of 'Another Sleep Song' is continued from 'Sleep Song' on his earlier solo album, both songs are probably for Joni. 'Miss You' with Graham sounding like Joni on piano must surely also be for Joni, it is one of Graham's simplest and most beautiful songs. There are other tracks which might be for Joni, if not then Graham's follow-up romance went the same way as had his and Joni's. 'Wild Tales' concerns a woman who has gone on the road, 'Hey You' concerns looking at the moon and dreaming. 'You'll Never Be the Same' has Graham reminding a woman that she will never be the same without him beside her. The front cover photograph shows Graham sitting with a book open at a photo of a tree, perhaps a reference to Joni's idea of trees ending their days in a museum. There are a pile of books close to Graham, the spine of one is clearly visible it states 'Goodbye Baby & Amen', a message to Joni perhaps. The photograph was taken by Joel Bernstein who pictured Joni naked for her 'For the Roses' cover. I must add that the album includes 'Prison Song' which is for Graham's father who was sent to prison for buying (or selling) a stolen camera at his place of work. He had no idea it was stolen, had no previous criminal record but was sent to prison which ultimately broke him, very sad, and extremely unfair when the rich can get away with just about anything. Joni's infatuation with that earlier Lambert, Hendricks and Ross album had remained within her psyche and now she decided to record her first all-electric and all jazz album. Using members of The Crusaders, C.S.N., L.A.Express and others she went into the studio with some great new songs.

COURT AND SPARK (released March 1974)

The cover was arresting and a little strange. The card cover was beige/yellow with the album title and Joni's signature written in marker-felt-tipped-pen around one of Joni's more surrealistic sketches. There are mountains behind a morass of 'foliage' that is sprouting up from the ground. This growth has two hands one with four fingers the other with three, they appear to be hugging a central stem. Painted in 1971 it is probably Joni in her Magritte/Dali/Picasso phase; Brian Hinton in his book thought it looked more like the style of Francis Bacon. Whatever it is supposed to depict it certainly is vague. The inside of the gatefold has a Norman Seef brightly illuminated photograph of a beautiful sensuous smiling Joni, the lighting has removed most of the face lines enhancing her nose and lips.

COURT AND SPARK: Joni says so much in this lyric. She speaks of the thrill of courtship regulated by the fear of emotional involvement with a drifter. She is ambivalent of this 'free love', she needs to trust him but there is no security which makes the courting even more exciting. It is easy for a drifter to suggest that she should sever all her inhibitions. Joni resists it all and we are left wondering if the attraction was not to a person but to her home in Canada, but she can't let go of Los Angeles. So is this a man suggesting that she leave with him and live elsewhere, or alternatively is it the attraction of going home? As you can observe it has taken me longer to explain the ambiguities than it takes Joni to present her lyric. His eyes were the colour of the sand and sea, he had sacrificed his blues, perhaps Joni was just not ready.

HELP ME: A song with a superb drum driven rhythm created by John Guerin, it is over laid by Larry Carlton's superb guitaring. Joni has rarely sung a song as well as this, she is falling in love again, this time with a drummer. She was resisting amorous advances in the previous track, here she is helpless and falling too fast. Because they both flirt and both need their respective freedom she is attempting to cope with it rather than submit to it. In her earlier song 'Cactus Tree' Joni was introducing the idea of the free woman, here that stance has crumbled away. In this song it is the man that wants to maintain his freedom, the best plans of all can be devastated by the arrival of true-love. The song is immediately appealing and remains one of my personal all time favourites from Joni, she certainly sounds as though she enjoyed singing it.

FREE MAN IN PARIS: This song has a similar loping beat to the previous track. Joni is slurring her vocal again, the slur is strangely alike to that of Steve Harley of Cockney Rebel fame. Joni is joined on this by Jose Feliciano and it has been alleged that this is a song for David Geffen. Joni seems to be relating a conversation she had with a man (Geffen ?) in Paris, or perhaps it is just Joni's imagination. This is not a song of love, it is a song of fame and the subsequent demands of that fame; trying to remain unfettered and alive.

PEOPLE'S PARTIES: Described in the Music Press as a Los Angeles party from hell. A party peopled by geriatrics, or are these people full of drugs? They are allowing themselves to succumb, not caring for themselves as well as they should. Joni is setting herself apart and observing the craziness. Annie Ross sung 'Fiesta in Blue' which presented the same scene, sad people crying and lying and attempting to comfort each other, although they are all in the same situation. Joni will have heard the song by Lambert Hendricks and Ross and might well have been the inspiration for this track. This song segues into...

....THE SAME SITUATION: An orchestral arrangement by Tom Scott for this song which is a study of ambition and the scars that result. Some heavy piano from Joni in the style of Procol Harum. This is the desire for a lasting love, possibly sung to James Taylor, the lyrics of a mixed-up woman who blames herself for not being able to accept the shortcomings of her man.

CAR ON A HILL: This sounds like a C.S.N.Y. song, we get musical doppler effects and changes in tempo, the choir inserted between the verses sound like some ladies from the canyon. The woman in the song is sitting in her car and waiting, he is already three hours late. This may just be an illusion, dreaming of the man who will never arrive. I wonder just how many women would wait for three hours? Joni also uses the word 'spark' again, I am sure she means it to be the ability to ignite love. 'Spark' also means witty (bright-spark) and a fashionable or gallant young man, they all fit the lyric adequately.

DOWN TO YOU: This song won a Grammy Award for Joni and Tom Scott, it was presented in March 1975 for 'Best Arrangement for a Vocalist'. Gene Puerling originally of the Hi Lo's was nominated in the same category twice with his 'Singers Unlimited'; Carol Shive and Esther Satterfield were the other unsuccessful nominee vocalists. This is the best love-gone song on the album but tackles an unsavoury subject. The man in the song picks-up prostitutes, and then returns home to his loneliness. Joni is almost re-using her 'Circle Game' scenario, everything comes full cycle, even opposites, brute to angel, crawl to fly, it comes and goes, a constant stranger. Nothing is permanent,

Leonard Cohen also wrote an enigmatic 'Stranger Song', here Joni repeats 'Constant Stranger', just when things seem perfect bad news comes knocking.

JUST LIKE THIS TRAIN: Apparently this is yet another song for James Taylor. This may be Joni answering the 'El lay' criticism from The Rolling Stone Magazine when she states that she used to count lovers like railroad cars. The protagonist in the song wanted enduring love, watching as his hair recedes, Taylor's has subsequently gone. In many of James Taylor's photographs he has arranged for the photographer to 'cut off' the top of the picture which shows his baldness, just look at his recent album covers. There is some great Larry Carlton guitar, as Joni uses her imagery to set the scene, she later admits that because she lost him she has resorted to self pity, she spitefully asks him "What are you going to do now that you've got no one to give your love to". Joni certainly exorcised a few of her ghosts on this lyric.

RAISED ON ROBBERY: A return to Lambert Hendricks and Ross for inspiration. One could confuse this with a The Band song especially as Robbie Robertson is included on the track. Watching Canadian hockey in the bar of The Empire Hotel. The 'lady' of the song forces her attentions on an unsuspecting male, she is soliciting for sex but not for free. This dispels the theory of Joni Mitchell appearing to be a vestal innocent, but of course this song is just fantasy and imagination. The attempt to pick the man up fails and she is lonely once more, back to the glass of gin.

TROUBLED CHILD: The story of a visit to someone in hospital who has overdosed on life? Is it insanity, an accident, drugs, we learn that he has been opened-up. He is lying in a room and the visitors don't really care, they are just a succession of visiting faces; this could be Joni's nightmare.

TWISTED (Ross/Grey): Trumpet leads us into the jazz vocalese classic, for some reason comedians Cheech and Chong are assisting, they were never known for their singing prowess. The song is special because it is the first non Joni Mitchell composed song that she had recorded. The song is of comedic insanity, great punch line at the end to explain the preceding schizophrenia. I am not privileged to know how many times Joni recorded this in the studio but surely she made a better fist of the song elsewhere. The song was written and sung originally by Annie Ross, Joni's performance pales into insignificance next to Annie's version. At least the album finishes with a smile, it needed it after the introversion of 'Troubled Child'

This became her most successful album, it went top ten in U.S.A. stalling at No 2, and No 14 in U.K. The sublime 'Help Me' reached No 7 in the U.S.A. singles listing. Jon Landau reviewing the album for Rolling Stone wrote 'On first listening this album is the first truly great pop album of 1974, sounds surprisingly light; by the third or fourth listening it reveals its underlying tensions'. Landau decided that.... 'Joni had an almost Zen-like dilemma, the freer the writer becomes, the more unhappy she finds herself; the more she surrenders her freedom the less willing she is to accept the resulting compromise'. Landau certainly had his finger on the pulse of Joni's work, she seemed to be destined to remain in the state of permanent dissatisfaction always knowing what she would like to do, always more depressed when it is done.

This review was prophetic in analysis, the last sentence would be a perfect description of Joni's career in sequence. She has composed so many songs filled with ambivalences, asking for change, approval, love, strength, but once she has these she does not feel happy. Landau completed his excellent review of the album by writing... 'The special beauty of 'Court and Spark' is that it forces us to both laugh and cry, and that it does so with such infinite grace'. To my mind a perfect description of almost a work of genius, a superb album.

Joni was now living in Bel Air in a 16 room house, almost certainly the plan view of the property and the swimming pool can be seen in the bottom left corner of 'The Hissing of Summer Lawns' cover.

A second single was taken from the album 'Free Man in Paris' with Jose Feliciano guesting, it only went as high as No 22. Joni was again touring in September 1974, Joni appeared at Wembley Stadium, London on a bill with The Band and C.S.N.Y.

During the days before Christmas Joni, Linda Ronstadt, James Taylor and his new wife Carly Simon busked along the streets of Los Angeles. One thing that must be said of Joni is that nearly all her love entanglements end with both participants remaining friends, a remarkable achievement.

MILES OF AISLES (1975)
THE HISSING OF SUMMER LAWNS (1976)

Hot can be cool and cool can be hot, and each can be both.
But hot or cool, man, jazz is jazz.
                                    Louis Armstrong (1900-1971)

Joni was preparing to release her first official live album. The live version of 'Big Yellow Taxi' was released as an appetizer and went to No 24 in the U.S.A. charts. The lyrics of the song had been updated from the 1970 version.

MILES OF AISLES (released February 1975)

This was a double live album of previously released songs but with two new songs included namely 'Jericho' and 'Love and Money'. The cover was half photograph half painting. Joni had expanded the picture by adding extra trees and some extra staging to both left and right of the 'miles of aisles'. The photograph is taken by Joni, her red-painted-toe-nails visible through open toed sandals are in the picture. Joni has also enhanced the roof acoustic panels by painting some of them in different colours. The lyrics of the two new songs are hand written by Joni, as are the band credits. A smiling band photo completes the cover, Joni and the L.A. Express. Henry Lewy who had been engineer for Joni since her second album is again in the chair, since David Crosby Produced the first album, production credits had not been given, and there are none on this album.

The recordings were taken from shows at The Universal Amphitheatre, over four days from August 14th 1974. One track 'Real Good For Free', (which is 'For Free' with an extra title prefix) was taken from Berkeley Community Centre earlier in March 1974. On this song Joni sounds as though she is likely to break into laughter at any time.

Just after Joni completes singing 'Cold Blue Steel and Sweet Fire' a member of the audience can be heard shouting 'Joni you have more class than Mick Jagger, Richard Nixon and Gomer Pyle U.S.M.C.'. This catches Joni unawares and she laughs in surprised enjoyment. Two of the protagonists are well known the third namely Gomer Pyle U.S.M.C. was in a situation comedy shown only in the U.S.A. Gomer was played by singer Jim Nabors who in the show was always having trouble with his Sergeant. U.S.M.C. refers to United States Marine Corps, Gomer Pyle is presented as a lovable underdog, he created the catch phrase 'handful of gimme and a mouthful of much obliged'. 'Was (Not Was)' group member Don Was and Elvis Costello wrote 'Shadow and Jimmy' for the 'What's Up Dog?' album, in that song they used a version of Pyle's phrase. According to Q Magazine's Question & Answer page, Jim Nabors was alleged to have been romantically linked to Rock Hudson.

JERICHO: To be Pedantic it was not Jericho that made the wall come tumbling down but Joshua. Here Joni is using those walls as her metaphor for her intellect that is obstructing a new love. She is attempting to open herself to love, it is obvious from the first line. The song is an open contract for another relationship. Joni is trying to learn from the past loves-lost and make all the necessary personal allowances, an exchange, another arrangement. Joni mentions wild dogs running free, and also refers to a Judas. For some reason unknown to me, this song and 'Love or Money' are not registered to Joni's Siquomb Music but Crazy Crow Music.

The Band also released an album titled 'Jericho' in 1993, it was their reunion album so many people assumed that it meant that the 'walls of opposition' had faded to make a new album. It was their first album of new material since 'Northern Lights' in 1975. Joshua's story states that the walls of Jericho fell down when seven ram's horns were blown and the people gave a mighty shout. The point is that if Joni uses the city as a metaphor for openness and The Band for their togetherness, it doesn't take much for either to crumble. Joni writes in her lyrics 'the dogs kennelled in me', dogs and wolves would feature later in her musical career.

LOVE OR MONEY: For the completist this track made the purchase essential, 'Jericho' would receive a studio treatment later, this was the only 'Love or Money' version available. Joni has handwritten the lyrics on the inner sleeve and spells 'demmands' incorrectly, probably for the purpose of pairing it with 'commands'. The song concerns the man who comes to Hollywood with his dreams of success, he has songs of love, songs of loss and of laughter. The second verse and the first half of the third verse is for 'Salome', or a woman like her. Finally this man arrives at Joni's house with an armful of balloons on strings, one should be attached to the moon for love, however he just couldn't manage it.

The album sold well, the advance orders meant that it got an extra impetus in the first week of availability. Although in the U.K. it only reached No 34, in the U.S.A. it reached the dizzy heights of No 2, following in the success of 'Court and Spark'. As mentioned earlier Tom Scott and Joni received a Grammy Award on March 1st for Best arrangement accompanying a vocalist. Joni also joined Bob Dylan's 'Rolling Thunder Revue' as a spectator but could not resist taking part at some of the shows. Bob was singing in white face make up at the time, the film 'Renaldo and Clara' resulted from these performances. Although Joni requested that she was not included within the film she can be observed in the background of some of the scenes. The film included David Blue, Joan Baez, Sara Dylan and many others; it has subsequently been acclaimed as a classic specialist film. In January 1976, Bob Dylan appeared unexpectedly at one of her shows in Austin, Texas. They duetted on 'Both Sides Now', then Bob sang 'Girl From the North Country', that was where Joni came from of course.

THE HISSING OF SUMMER LAWS (released January 1976)

The album's cover was extremely eye-catching. The 'hissing' of the title refers to the hoses and sprinklers watering the lawns of the affluent residents of Los Angeles. It is pertinent to understand that one can't travel far inland from the Californian coast before encountering desert. I am not sure if the hissing is additionally used as a title because the hoses connecting the sprinklers would appear like hissing snakes across those lawns. The cover is green in the forward areas and silver for the sky and buildings. The houses of some imaginary Canadian town stretch across the gatefold, one has sky blue board facias and a car. Set behind these dwellings as a back drop is a New York city-scape of high rise properties. The original cover was expensive to produce as it was embossed. The five African men and a boy on the cover are carrying an anaconda towards a chapel set upon the side of a hill. To the bottom left of this panorama is Joni's Bel Air home complete with sky blue swimming pool. It is set incongruously in green belt isolated and scarring the countryside. Joni also provides some notes concerning the album which are written above a photo of Joni lazing in her swimming pool. She takes time to thank 'Helpful Henry the housewives delight' which may be the odd-job man but is more likely 'H' for heroin, or perhaps cocaine. It might in fact be quite innocently, extra thanks for Henry Lewy who with the assistance of Ellis Sorkin mixed and engineered the album. Joni also thanks parents Myrt (Myrtle) and Bill Anderson in North Battleford, which is a town approximately 100 miles from Saskatoon in Saskatchewan State, Canada. Joni's latest lover, John Guerin, is thanked for showing Joni the 'root of the chord and where I was'.

It was reported that the swimming pool photograph of Joni irritated friend Neil Young into writing the song 'Stupid Girl', he included it on his 'Zuma' album. It is more likely that the picture inspired Neil to write the song, it might not have been for Joni at all. The 'stupid Girl' is a 'beautiful fish', and Neil's criticism was probably due to Joni criticising non-jazz musicians (of which

Neil was one) of not being competent to play her new music. In Neil's song the stupid girl has a lot to learn. One wonders if Neil's 'Zuma' album sleeve design was also aimed at Joni, it is a pencil sketch with a 'Cactus Tree' and a stork that looks more like a 'Seagull' which is carrying a naked young woman. The cover was also a sketch which seemed to require colouring-in as did a couple of Joni's album sleeves.

Joni was receiving disapproval for her over-bearing and swollen headed attitude, apparently if a person was not famous then she would not talk to them. I am of course reporting gossip and tittle-tattle here, but journalists Nick Kent and Barney Hoskyns' both mentioned it at the time. Joni was also responding to audience heckling badly, getting upset and aggressive with on stage verbal retaliation. As she was known to 'have-a-go' back at the audience if they made a noise, the audiences did it more and more. Joni then started cancelling dates, in fact she became extremely unreliable, and booking agents willing to take a chance on her appearing (or not) became fewer and fewer.

In earlier albums Joni used the first person stance of 'I', it has become 'You' on many of the tracks on the 'Hissing' album. The album has less personal confession and more philosophy, Joni has selected many American social stereotypes, the materialists, the pseudo-realists with their freedom restricted by their need to possess. She has included them in scenes in her songs which become ritual dramas with an underlying view on feminism. Steely Dan's, Jeff Skunk Baxter, plays guitar and adds his easily recognisable sound. The Jazz Crusaders, Larry Carlton, Joe Sample and Wilton Felder are again present as are Max Bennett, John Guerin, Robben Ford and Victor Feldman of the L.A.Express, but for some reason L.A.Express leader Tom Scott is absent.

IN FRANCE THEY KISS ON MAIN STREET: The backing vocals on this jazzy song are from David Crosby, Graham Nash and James Taylor, all ex-lovers in harmony with each other and Joni. This is very similar to 'Help Me' from 'Court and Spark', this is the song of two women Gail and Louise out dancing in their younger days, wearing their push-up-brassieres. Back in the days of Marlon Brando's biker films, everything seemed to be much less complicated. The scene created by Joni could be taken from the film 'Grease', everyone looking for a party, kissing was as far as passion went, but they were also rock 'n' rolling!

THE JUNGLE LINE: The drums used for the backing track are taken from Nonesuch Explorer Series and this is credited on the rear of the cover. Burundi Black Stevenson also used the track to make a brilliant single. Debbie Harry and Blondie used a similar rhythm on 'Orchid Club' and Paul Simon polished the sound for many on his percussive influenced albums. The drum recording on Joni's track was made in Burundi for the French Government ethnic musical archives in 1967. Joni has changed one word from the lyric sheet, she sings 'screaming' in a ritual of sound, the written word is 'burning'. The drums certainly provide a dazzling back-drop for this song. The lyric is Joni's interpretation of a painting by Henri Rousseau. Rousseau was known as 'Douanier' (customs house officer) which was his full time occupation. He was an amateur painter, his tropical scenes are all imagined. He served in tropical America (Mexico) during his military service and used these memories to create his 'African' scenes. Rousseau would paint a nude figure on a couch in the depth of an imaginary jungle, or a mass of flowers and plants and call it 'The Equatorial Jungle'. Joni here describes various paintings, Rousseau also painted scenes of Paris but I don't think he did one of The Brooklyn Bridge. This is a great track that found me putting the stylus back a couple of times for a replay, even in 1998. Joni of course couldn't resist slipping in a few ambiguities like smuggled powder, slaving boats, and the point of the song becomes suddenly apparent it is the vanishing forests, the onward advance of the 'jungle line'.

EDITH AND THE KINGPIN: This is a nice lilting song with a sting in the tail, Joni lulls us with the tune into a false sense of security. This song is just like the meeting in Steely Dan's 'Haitian Divorce'. The king pin or the big man attracts the ladies, he is also friends with the police. He sees Edith, he can't wait to get hold of her. His women age very quickly because he teaches them to take drugs from a small spoon. They are snowblind (snow is slang for white powder drugs), this is the awful seduction of the soul. So has Edith succumbed and become a prostitute under Kingpin's control, he never takes his eyes off her, its all a surrealistic nightmare.

DON'T INTERRUPT THE SORROW: Joni claims this to be a poem first, and a song second. She stated that the song was born at 4.00am in a New York loft by Larry Poons who 'seeded' it and Bob Neuwirth who was the midwife. Joni also admits to taking it as her immaculate conception and claiming it as her own. The lyric has the trepidation of her anima rising. Anima is extracted from Jungian philosophy 'the inner personality', but more often it refers to feminine thoughts within the male's unconscious thoughts. Confused, there's more. She has not been controlled by a man but seems to agree that alcohol has dominated her. The mystery becomes even more impenetrable as the lyric unfolds. The first verse sets the scene of the drinking session, then the anima rises within 'her', which is somewhat bizarre. Joni then points her finger at the patriarchal society, but the protagonist here has been free since the age of seventeen. A discussion follows in verse five, the drinking continues, the women are subjugated, masculine myths of power will fall as soon as the man becomes weak. Without reading the lyric the track just passes by as filler, but I wonder if my analysis is correct, as Joni says in the song "A rebel loves a cause!"

SHADES OF SCARLETT CONQUERING: Scarlett O'Hara, 'Gone with the Wind', beautiful ballroom gowns, Errol Flynn and Clark Gable, the scene is set. Watching the film unfold, living in the deep south of America. Scarlett has gentle hands and red fingernails. The song is of a girl seeing the film and attempting to be Scarlett O'Hara and hoping that one day she will 'have everything'. But what is Errol Flynn doing in 'Gone With the Wind'?

THE HISSING OF SUMMER LAWNS: This is for housewives everywhere. Married to a rich man living the comfortable existence where she has everything she needs, but it is all so boring. The rich live in big houses with barbed wire perimeter fences, they pretend to be happy, or as Joni puts it "wear a joyful mask'. The lawns hiss with hose-pipes, they spend money on jewellery for the dog. She has antique furniture that no-one sits in, financially happy but emotionally starved; but of course this might just be Joni herself. Laying in her swimming pool listening to the hoses, remember John Guerin was showing her the 'root of the chord' at the time.

THE BOHO DANCE: On the sleeve notes Joni says that this is a 'Tom Wolfe-ism' from the book 'Painted Word'. Tom Wolfe, the new journalism, fashion and the preening male in his white suit. The credibility of the bohemian lifestyle, no glamour for the beatnik. The reason why Joni was interested in the book is due to the connection between 'the word' and the pseudo 'art world'. Real art experts are few and far between, the whole painting scene pretends that it is not commercialised when it is part of the impenetrable establishment tenets. In the lyric Joni is presenting her opinion of the commercialised fashion scene, after all she was part of the art scene herself, a 'name' sells paintings much easier than talent. So called art experts were recently fooled into hailing as brilliant, paintings performed by chimpanzees using celery stalks as brushes. I particularly like the inference in Joni's lyric where she states that 'a priest has a pornographic watch, but looks longingly to the sky', what for divine intervention?

HARRY'S HOUSE-CENTREPIECE (Johnny Mandel/Jon Hendricks): I thought the song was also co-composed by Harry Sweets Edison, but I may be wrong, the song was registered in 1958. Edison recorded the track with Jimmy Forrest years ago, as did John Coltrane and Coleman Hawkins, the lyric may have been added to Edison's solo. Of course Harry's house may be Harry Edison's. This song was also sung regularly by Joni's favourite trio of Lambert, Hendricks and Ross. The song is an eternal favourite of Van Morrison who often includes it in his live shows. Van Morrison used the services of Georgie Fame in his band in the 1990s, Georgie had a number one hit with Jon Hendricks' 'Yeah Yeah'. Centrepiece is sung from the standpoint of Harry, it evolves into song of female emancipation, the husband is out working and becomes the wife's slave. She is materially comfortable but emotionally starved again, the same thought appeared in the earlier 'Hissing' song. On this occasion Joni presents an alternative and she leaves him, showing just what she could achieve with Harry's money, and his house. I love the description of the helicopter landing on the Pan Am roof like 'a dragonfly on a tomb', sublime poetic Mitchell; she also catches the man and 'reels him in'. Joe Sample plays a jazz solo on piano, Chuck Finlay's muted trumpet follows alongside the vocal, Joni's voice acquires some added reverb as she talks to Harry. Joni also modifies the song from the lyric sheet when she sings 'Yellow school of taxi fishes' rather than 'taxi schools of yellow fishes', there seems no reason for the amendment.

SWEET BIRD: Joni and Larry Carlton alone on this track. This is the 'Sweet Bird of Youth' which was a play by Tennessee Williams. In that play a Hollywood drifter brings an ageing glamour star back to his home town, but encounters revenge from the father of a girl he had seduced. In the film the woman was Geraldine Page the drifter Paul Newman and the father Ed Begley, Begley received an Oscar for his performance. Joni on the song mentions vanity and the promises of youth from a jar. Time marches on laughing at the sadness of those people chasing eternal youth.

SHADOWS AND LIGHT: This is a staccato chant, African in style, the first verse sung a-cappella, synthesizer augments later. Joni is moralising in this stream of consciousness writing style, almost sermonizing. Judges, mythical Gods and Devils, Governments, parasites, the necessity to decide what is wrong and what is right. The song is more 'blindness' and light than shadows, but the meaning of it all remains obscured and threatened by the light. The overall sentiment seems to be that men are frauds and women are far stronger mentally.

'In France They Kiss on Main Street' was released as a single but only reached No 66 in U.S.A. Stephen Holden's review of the album in The

Rolling Stone in January 1976 did not hint at what that magazine intended to write later concerning the album. Holden did write that the album... 'offers substantial literature, it is set to insubstantial music. There are no tunes to speak of'. He went on to find that... 'Joni's interest in melody had become increasingly eccentric relying on elaborate production and lyrics, hence her growing interest in jazz'. Holden also thought that... 'the synthesizer on 'Shadows and Light'... 'sounds like a long solemn fart', whatever that sounds-like. Holden concluded his quite reasonable review by writing... 'If Joni intends to experiment further with jazz she ought to work with an artists of her own stature, someone like Keith Jarrett whose jazz-classical compositions are spiritually and romantically related to Joni Mitchell's best work'. Holden concluded his review by stating....'this 'Hissing' album is ultimately a great collection of pop poems with a distracting soundtrack-read it first-then play it'. The Rolling Stone Magazine seemed to have some form of vendetta against Joni. After the unforgivable promiscuous family tree they added salt to the wound by voting the 'Summer Lawns' album the 'Worst' album of the year. Perhaps they could have added the epithet 'by a major artist'; curiously their Rolling Stone reviewer Stephen Holden had written... 'great collection of pop poems with a distracting soundtrack'. The lyrics were certainly Joni's most complex, it is also fair to report that the majority of the reviews considered the album poor. In hindsight nearly all Joni fans seem to like the album, a slow starter that has grown in favour over the years. To countermand the Rolling Stone Magazine's accolade of 'worst album' both New Musical Express (NME) and Sounds music papers in the U.K. voted 'Hissing' their 'Best Album of the Year'. I personally think it is excellent.

HEJIRA (1976)

> *Let us sing on our journey as far as we go;*
> *the way will be less tedious.*
>
> Virgil (70-19BC)

Joni and John Guerin separated, another relationship had failed. Joni decided to travel around the USA in a car, incognito. She travelled from New York to Los Angeles writing songs as she travelled. It seems that her time with the 'Rolling Thunder Revue' had allowed her to see at first hand the egotism of the stars involved. At the same time of course journalists were remarking on the arrogance and snobbishness of Joni herself. Due to travelling with her guitar the 'Hejira' album is devoid of piano songs, in fact there are never more than four musicians on any one track. As Joni was making her attempt to escape from her failed relationship by travelling, she curiously compared it to the escape of Mohammed from Mecca to Medina in the year 622, the commencement of The Muslim era, his Hejira (usually written as Hegira); Hejira also symbolises 'escaping with honour'.

HEJIRA (released November 1976)

The album is again jazz oriented, and Jaco Pastorius' bass playing glows throughout the album. Jaco was known to be a difficult musician, he had great confidence in his musicianship which was certainly justified, but this was interpreted by many as arrogance. I first heard Joni's album when John Peel played it complete without interruptions on his Top Gear programme on the evening of 23rd November 1976. As I had recorded the programme it saved me the problem of buying it, I wonder how many others could say the same. I still have that John Peel programme (and many others) which I regularly play in my car. Peel loved the album and just wanted us to hear it immediately, I am not sure if Asylum Records would have been very pleased. It did however sell very well in the U.K. reaching No 11 in December 1976, and in the USA rising to No 13. In his introduction John Peel quoted from Tim Lott's review of the album from that week's Sounds Music Weekly. Tim Lott had written....

> 'Hejira is timeless and majestic, this is music for the spirit,
> Intellectual and inspired, this is music for the mind.
> Rhythmic and subtle, this is music for the body,
> The music of tomorrow, this is the tip of the iceberg.
> Don't hear this album, listen to it.

John Peel agreed with Tim Lott and so do I.

The Hejira cover is beautiful, it comprises a series of photographs merged rather than collaged. Joni at her most striking, her hair billowing to her right (as in nearly all her photographs), she is smoking a cigarette. Her hands are floating in the nothingness of a long straight road, the clouds on the horizon soar up into Joni's imitation fur coat. Joni's portrait by Norman Seef is set into a full frozen lake landscape taken by Joel Bernstein. There are trees to the right and to the left in a surrealistic scene, a male ice skater in his one piece stretch suit poses in front of a girl in her wedding dress. The inside photo shows Joni skating holding her arms horizontal, her coat (or scarf) hangs down like the feathers of some giant black bird.

There is a change to the band credits for this album, Joni has decided to call herself just 'Mitchell'. Jaco Pastorius adds bass to four of the seven tracks that have a bass, Max Bennett plays on two and Chuck Domanico on one. Larry Carlton (guitar), Victor Feldman (vibraphone), John Guerin (drums), Bobbye Hall (percussion) are also present. Abe Most plays clarinet on 'Hejira' and Neil Young adds harmonica on 'Furry Sings the Blues'. After fullness of the sound of the previous album the listener soon becomes aware just how sparse the backings are, here they punctuate rather than accompany.

COYOTE' The first words on this song (and the album of course) are 'No Regrets'. Perhaps Joni is the coyote that has left home and gone out searching for life, a viable reason for the title. A coyote bites the nose of its baby and sends it out into the world to fend for itself. It was mooted at the time that song was directed at Warren Beatty. Joni uses sing-speak for the vocal here, the playing of Jaco Pastorius and Larry Carlton is a superb backdrop. The man in question has a ranch and a wife and another woman, or women. Joni is on the road a prisoner of the white lines. They drive past a burning farmhouse, the man tracks her down and soon they are dancing. Later in the song we become aware that other men she meets are also considered to be coyotes. She is wrestling with her ego and his flame seems to be the point of the song, a separation to sort things out. A superb song to open the album.

AMELIA: The journey continues, the thoughts turning to Amelia Earhart who was the first woman to fly across the Atlantic as a passenger in 1928 (Newfoundland-Wales), and again in 1932 (Newfoundland-Northern Ireland) solo. Whilst attempting to fly across the Pacific she disappeared. The drone of the aeroplanes on Joni's journey brought Amelia to her mind. The Cactus Tree Motel is the situation for her song, strange that 'Cactus Tree' should return. Icarus is also mentioned as an alternative aviator. Apart from Icarus' foolish flight to the sun with waxen wings, he, according to folklore, made other wings and flew from Crete to other islands in the Grecian archipelago. Joni declares that she has spent her life in the clouds at icy attitudes, in the Motel she continues to miss the object of her affections, the man from whom she is making her escape.

FURRY SINGS THE BLUES; When Joni visited Furry Lewis he said that he hated the song, he added that he didn't like Joni either, in his mind she had stolen his soul. Seems more than a little ungrateful to me, more people will remember Furry through this song than anything that he recorded. Neil Young back in Joni's good books less than a year after he wrote 'Stupid Girl' about her, plays harmonica supposedly in the style of Furry Lewis. Joni is now in the Deep South in Memphis, W.C. Handy's statue and Beale Street. Furry Lewis has had a leg amputated and is in hospital. The town seems to be run-down, shops closed, a town in decay, Joni's shiny limousine seems incongruous in Furry's shanty street. Walter Furry Lewis first recorded in 1928, it was 1958 before he recorded again when he was re-discovered. Furry was part of the Dr Willie Lewis Medicine Show, with Gus Cannon and Will Shade, they entertained the crowds whilst Dr Lewis sold his 'Jack rabbit salve'. The earlier mentioned W.C. Handy's statue was absurdly placed in a park very close to the toilets, hence the pun there's always a WC Handy. 'Gus Cannon' wrote 'Walk Right In' a big hit for The Rooftop Singers.

A STRANGE BOY: Observations from the car as a boy passes on a yellow skateboard. This is possibly a boy with learning difficulties, or perhaps a man tied to his mothers apron strings. The boy certainly is happy with his lot, he does not wish to grow up. The last verse becomes another of Joni's nightmares. More 'Tales of Hoffman' memories, glass eyes staring, antique dolls in a cellar, and the sudden memories of illicit love in a dormitory; with the same boy who would not grow up? Of course Joni might be using the whole scenario as a metaphor for the last man in her life, prior to her hejira.

HEJIRA: This song does not have a constructed melody, it all seems to be improvised behind Joni's vocal. Abe Most plays his clarinet to represent Benny Goodman (mentioned in the song) for a few seconds then leaves the album completely. The first verse is Joni coming to terms with the possessiveness of the relationship, they had reached the pinnacle where they could 'thaw or freeze'. It seems that Joni has decided that the relationship is over, under the millions of stars all her problems have been minimalised.

SONG FOR SHARON: This is the longest track on the album, sung to a tune slightly similar to the M*A*S*H theme, possibly it should have been 'Song to Sharon' as it is written in the style of a letter or diary. Joni is reminiscing of her younger days back in Canada, buying her ukulele (mandolin), a wedding dress in a shop window, Red Indian children playing. Each verse adds to the story, gambling, emotions, paying $18 to see a gypsy, leaving her man and travelling to New York, committing suicide in a muddy well, ecology-skating, attending other girls' weddings, they all pass before us in a stream of consciousness. Joni is in an ambivalence between having a family life and the life of singing star, yet she makes the lyric ambiguous by cleverly reversing the last verse. Through all the unwanted advice from Dora, Mama and Betsy, Joni decides what she really wants is another lover.

BLACK CROW: Joni resembles a crow in the skating photograph on the inner of the gatefold, her arms outstretched and her scarf hanging down like wings. Poet and writer Ted Hughes wrote 'Crow the Scavenger', here the crow is a metaphor for Joni's troubled soul. A face with 'crows feet', a haggard face in a bathroom mirror. A crow is a gregarious songbird, just like Joni. A crow is like an old and ugly woman, which is not like Joni, but she seems to think she looks that way in the mornings.

BLUE MOTEL ROOM: She has reached a hotel room in Savannah. Joni has come to terms with herself and after visiting two dozen American States she is on her way home to 'him' in Los Angeles. Now she contemplates the situation she might find when she gets there. The mind boggles at the thought of his 'boom-boom-pachyderm', whatever that is? A pachyderm is a very thick skinned animal, an elephant, who is it representing? Joni is ready to atone, a blue hotel room for the blues.

REFUGE OF THE ROADS: Joni had found shelter and protection on the roads. This track is like some Kerouacian over-view of the journey, the people the places, the analysis, the dreams the blues. Joni observes a photograph of The Earth taken from the Moon and continues to realise how insignificant her problems really are. Westbound and rolling she is on her way home. This ends a superb album enhanced by some of the best bass playing Jaco Pastorius ever achieved.

When I first heard the album back in 1976 I was not sure about it, now 22 years later it stands out as a massive accomplishment of superb lyrics and minimalist arrangements, everyone involved seemed to be at their creative peak, it sounds better now than ever. More music-as-therapy was the way that the album was reviewed at the time, a woman making private sense of her own experience. The title of the album must have been Joni's way of expressing her own escape from the accessibility of 'Court and Spark', here she is flirting with us, the listeners, again. The consensus of opinion was that Joni was not bothering with melodies, she was more interested in getting her philosophical point across. She was using a single line refrain to add a memorable 'hook' to the songs in lieu of a melody. Joni is travelling and composing, she wants to be loved, she want the accolades of being a singer and songwriter, but she is at least aware that the separations caused by the life-style are emotionally divisive, it is here in the songs, 'Coyote' and 'Blue Motel Room', both approached in a different style, acceptance and drollery. Ariel Swartley in Rolling Stone concluded perfectly that 'Joni makes no glib conclusions, it is her uncertainly, the alternating warmth and chill, which is most fascinating, she is never complacent; it is not the answers that are most important but the search itself'.

Bob Dylan was singing in aid of Hurricane Carter, a boxer that had been imprisoned for murder. Bob Dylan thought that he had suffered from rough justice and was campaigning for his release. Joni was not so sure, and she was proved correct when after Carter was released he was soon involved and convicted of another assault and was re-incarcerated. If there was a problem between Joni, Neil Young and Tom Scott (he was not on the 'Hissing' album), then it was all forgotten as they both joined Joni back on stage. Joni also joined John Sebastian, Fred Neil and Country Joe McDonald on stage in a 'Save the Whales' concert at The Memorial Auditorium, Sacramento, California. Country Joe was becoming extremely ecology conscious in his songs, in fact he released a whole album of 'Save this and save that songs' called 'Animal Tracks'.

The Band had decided to separate and they had their farewell concert titled 'The Last Waltz' at The Winterland, San Francisco. Joni sang 'Helpless' with Neil Young, 'Coyote' with Dr John and joined in the 'I Shall Be Released' all star finale. A film was also made of the show by Martin Scorsese, a live-show film with interviews and 'fly on the wall' gossip sessions. Joni also was on backing vocals for 'Arcadian Driftwood' and sang 'Shadows and Light' and 'Furry sings the Blues' but they were not used in the film. The elusive world 'ringolevio champion' and famous San Francisco digger Emmett Grogan introduced a song, but no one can remember him being there, or can they?

DON JUAN'S RECKLESS DAUGHTER (1978)

A verbal art like poetry is reflective, it stops to think.
Music is immediate; it goes on to become.
                                                W.H.Auden (1907-1973)

Joni now had a relationship with another drummer, this time Don Alias. Don Alias is an excellent drummer he was also present on Jaco Pastorius' brilliant eponymously titled first album. Joni had also met Weather Report saxophonist Wayne Shorter, he was to remain in her band of musicians for many years to come. Joni had travelled to Rio Janeiro to see the Carnival and she claimed that the album title reflects the love she felt there.

There are many Don Juan's in fiction, not all are great beguiling lovers as portrayed by Errol Flynn. Brian Hinton in his book 'Both Sides Now' located a book where Carlos Castaneda a graduate of UCLA meets a Yacqui Indian named Don Juan, there are other Juans. Don Juan Tenorio written by Jose Zorrilla, is the most popular conception for the character. Zorrilla re-worked the original legend, the wicked rake and Cynical sensualist Don Juan is finally saved from the fires of hell by falling in love with the pure virginal Dona Ines. Although Juan prays to God for forgiveness, God actually listens to Dona. Don Juan is also the leading character in 'Love Rogue' by Tirso de Molina (real name Gabriel Tellez). Don Juan in this book is a young noble, a rake, gambler and a blasphemer. In this tale Juan goes from one woman to another making promises he has no intention of keeping. This we had learned earlier from Joni was her idea of masculine morals. The Molina version has a surrealistic ending when Don Juan pulls the beard of a statue of a man he has killed earlier and invites him to dinner. The statue duly arrives at the appointed hour and offers his hand to Juan, as he takes hold of it Juan is consumed by hellfire. Finally George Bernard Shaw in 'Man and Superman' took his ideas from Nietzsche and made Don Juan a revolutionist in love with a moral; Shaw called his Juan, John Tanner, it is in a dream that he becomes Don Juan. The play moralises on the Life Force versus the Devil, and the winner is.....

If Joni considers herself Don Juan's reckless daughter then that leaves her father Bill Anderson as Don Juan. With all this rhetoric put aside, the probable Don Juan in Joni's heart was new lover Don Alias, it may have been as simple as that.

DON JUAN'S RECKLESS DAUGHTER (released January 1978)

A double album in a truly awful cover. Joni in black-face and moustache holding a medal on a ribbon, she is dressed in a man's three piece suit. Three seagulls fly upwards, there is another photograph of Joni wearing a dress which has teddy bears and a naked woman (breasts and pubic hair) printed on it. A young lad approaches from the right hand side looking downwards. On the rear there is a picture of Joni as a child wearing a blanket and hat and carrying a tom-tom drum , she looks like a young Red Indian girl. Another seagull is flying above the horizon. These pictures are set on a dark brown printed cover, above the horizon the sky is green. Joni in black-face has a speech balloon saying the albums title, Joni the Indian is saying 'How', we the album buyers were looking at this monstrosity saying 'why?' The same colours are taken over into the gatefold, the lyrics set on the brown areas and more seagulls are flying from the green sky. As if this was not enough the inner bags carry these colours also. On one side 'black-face' (and black wigged) Joni is saying "Mooslems, Moooslems! Heh Heh Heh" (her spelling not mine), and the Joni in a dress (now without the bears and the nude print) is saying 'Baila Mi Rumba'. The other bag has Joni in dress standing with her back to us looking at a floating red teddy bear balloon, the bear similar to the type on the cover dress. Here she is saying 'In My Dweems We Fwy'.

The complete double album played for just over an hour, if Todd Rundgren could get 30 minutes of music each side of 'A Wizard a True Star' then why not Joni Mitchell. What compounds this felony is that the compact disc was also released as a double. The reviews were mixed, The Rolling Stone Magazine's Janet Maslin said Joni sounded 'drowsy and disengaged'.

It did reach No 20 in the UK and No 25 in the USA, it gave Joni yet another Gold Record, her eighth.

OVERTURE-COTTON AVENUE: Jaco's growling bass lines for a stream of consciousness lyric. After the lack of a tune on the superb 'Hejira' it comes as a surprise that we have a melody. Cotton Avenue sounds like a good place to go for an evening out. The boys are outside looking tough, the girls are inside a dance hall enjoying themselves. This is their special place whatever happens outside they are lost in their own private world of pleasure.

TALK TO ME: An up-tempo song punctuated by Jaco Pastorius' bass just as on the previous album. I think that this track might have been remaindered from 'Hejira' it would certainly have fitted comfortably within that album's environment. Joni (if it is Joni) becomes loose-tongued when she is drunk. She wants to talk to her mystery man about anything, she lists some of the subjects up for debate in the lyric. Joni uses some poetic license when she writes 'slings and arrows of outrageous 'romance''. She is drunk and urinating the full length of a car park, smitten perhaps by Don Alias. Debbie Pead in Record Collector said she found this song 'outrageously brilliant', and I agree. She continues as a gabbling drunk at a party imploring at the finale to be shut-up by him taking his turn to talk to her. A song for feeling embarrassed at her alcohol based bravado, if he did speak to her would she be able to remember it tomorrow anyway?

JERICHO: Premiered live on 'Miles of Aisles', this is the studio version. Here we have a lovers and ex-lovers percussion section with both Don Alias and John Guerin playing. Joni only changes two words from the original version, here she sings 'let all these dogs' (previously 'and all the dogs'), and more pertinently 'I need that too' was previously 'I need that from you too'. Wayne Shorter adds soprano saxophone, he would be in Joni's entourage for some time to come. Shorter was originally playing tenor saxophone as a member of Art Blakey's band, he was there from 1959 to 1963. In 1964 he joined Miles Davis where Shorter started playing soprano saxophone. In 1970 Shorter created Weather Report with Joe Zawinul, in 1977 he toured with his V.S.O.P. Band which comprised the 'old' Miles Davis band of Herbie Hancock, Tony Williams, Ron Carter with the addition of Freddie Hubbard in place of Miles Davis.

PAPRIKA PLAINS: A long song at 16 minutes which takes up the full second side of the double album. Michael Gibbs is called on to provide the orchestration. Michael Gibbs recorded four lauded albums in the early 1970s, which command high prices in the specialist used-record shops. He worked with Gary Burton and Neil Ardley on jazz albums, his 'Just Ahead' double album is regarded as a classic. Paprika is red pepper, the colour of the sandy land. A panorama mixed with thoughts as viewed from above from a helicopter. She feels stifled in her present location and needs to return home to where people rely on the weather for everything. She thinks back to 1946 and McGee's General Store and the dancing Red Indians. The Red Indians traded beads for alcohol and the railway was built, surely that was before 1946? This pastoral scene of days controlled by daylight rather than the city clock, the Red Indians have lost all they ever had, except their dignity.

Joni moves the plot away to Hiroshima and the Atomic bomb, viewing the Earth from space. Joni adds the perforated blinds that she recalls were hung above her crib, this is known to be her first memory as a child. Joni is creating a surrealistic film in words, painting pictures that gradually change, a beach ball as a globe of the world and the puncturing of it with her fingernail, it then changes into a mirrored ball. This particular Red Indian's tipple is J & B (Justerini and Brooks) and coke, Joni is dreaming it all as if she were on the astral-plane having left her body. The ordinary things of mundane pastoral life are important, in the orchestration we hear piano and strings against the heavy chord structure of bass and drums, they are sounding the death knell for the inhabitants of the paprika plains. A great and powerful lyric of nostalgia, things were always better then, but were they? On one of the cover's inner-bags Joni stands in a paprika plain and the speech balloon says 'In my dweems we fwy', a child reminisces.

OTIS AND MARLENA: Miami, a Hades filled with old and retired tourists that pour into the city for fun and sun. Miami is also a parade ground for the women with their surgically adjusted bodies. At The Miami Royal Hotel, Marlena is white and sophisticated, Otis is golden brown and although on holiday he continues watching television. It would take a painter like Joni to use 'flake' for 'white' in the lyric, 'flake white' is a pigment made from flakes of white lead. The underlying message seems to be that whilst their homes are empty Muslims stick-up Washington, what does she mean?

THE TENTH WORLD (instrumental): This track is written by Joni's band, a studio jam session by the sound of it. If this 'melody' is registered the lead sheet must have taken some considerable time to write, it even has five nondescript vocals, Chaka Khan is there just humming on this track, Manolo Badena is on 'lead' vocal, the others are answering back to his call. This track becomes 7 minutes of meandering nonsense, the complete third side of the album with this track included is still just 15 minutes long.

DREAMLAND: Joni sang this on Bob Dylan's Rolling Thunder Review. Roger McGuinn then recorded 'Dreamland' on his solo 'Cardiff Rose' album released in June 1976. Another of Joni's percussive tracks, the lyric is the converse of the scenario presented in Otis and Marlena. This is an Utopia of goodness and light, interrupted by the explorers taking over America, interrupted by Salvationists trumpeting their message. The snow on Joni's mother Myrtle's lawn intersperses the scenario of a woman who has found her dream 'Marlboro Man'. Wherever the civilization reaches they sit there in their reclining chairs and await dreamland. Joni may allude to 'The Gates of Dreams' of which in ancient mythology there are two. The Ivory Gate which allows the dreams of delusion to pass through, the other The Gate of Horn which allows only the dreams that come true to pass through.

DON JUAN'S RECKLESS DAUGHTER: I thought it was The Pretenders as Joni sounds like Chrissie Hynde. The lyric was evidently set in motion by Joni seeing a television programme on U.S.A. Channel 5. In the earlier verses Joni is coming to terms with her 'serpent', her temptation, such as whisky bars and romance; or is the serpent a man telling her lies. The man is similar to Joni, yet she vehemently calls him a coward caught between yes-and-no. Joni realises that she is a coward too, I suppose the eagle represents Joni's pure and good thoughts. This is one of Joni's finest ambiguous lyrics, at the end of the turmoil created in the words Joni explains that the eagle represents feathers self denial and woman, the serpent is scales self indulgence and man. I thought men were snaps and snails and puppy dog tails, this is Joni's version. In the band credits Joni has added 'The split tongued spirit, El Bwyd', now who might that be, a Byrd perhaps.

OFF-NIGHT BACKSTREET: Augmented by J.D.Souther and Glenn Frey on backing vocals, their addition is bland, it could be anyone. If Mike Gibbs provided an orchestration for this track where is it? A song for her latest lost man, loving without trusting seems a dangerous course to take, it breeds jealousy. He has moved in with another woman, at night-time she thinks of him. At the coda we learn that she has a man on stand-by, but who left their long 'black' hair in the bathtub drain?

THE SILKY VEILS OF ARDOR: The final track, Joni is a lost soul floating in her dreams. Joni returning to the style of her first two albums, the idea of romantic visions of love. Ardor (ardour) are feelings of great intensity and warmth, eagerness and zeal, but this does not present itself in the lyric. This is just Joni and her guitar, she is still living in the hope of finding that perfect man. In dreams we fly, the woman; in dweems we fwy, the child. Perhaps the question remains in the child's voice balloon on the rear of the cover 'How?'. A good double album that would have been a great single album, this album has improved with age.

This album completed a trilogy for Joni Mitchell. 'The Hissing of Summer Lawns' was her African album, 'Hejira' her Arabic-Islamic album and 'Don Juan' is inspired by South America, all this produced years before Paul Simon decided to do it. Janet Maslin writing for the Rolling Stone decided that the best that could be said for the album was she had gambled and lost, it was in her opinion an instructive failure. she continues by writing... 'She has tried to incorporate jazz and calypso rhythms that eventually overpower her.' The consensus of opinion of the time (and Maslin's) was that the double album should have been a single album selecting the better tracks. The double is sapped of emotion and full of ideas that should have remained whims, melodies that should have remained riffs, songs that should have been fragments. To me this just sounded like nit-picking, after all the Rolling Stone had hardly been kind to Joni, she was always set up to be knocked down.

Joni's talents were stretched on these albums that is true, she may have been short of material to record and thus she decided to expand some of the songs, the title track for one would have been better at half the length. Janet Maslin concludes with 'She's bound to be back when the time is right and the mood less drowsy, less disengaged than it seems here. Until then we're left with Don Juan's Daughter, in all its recklessness'.

Joni's band and Mike Gibbs all assisted Jaco Pastorius with his solo album, released in 1976, it remains a classic, only Charlie Haden and Charles Mingus to my mind, have managed to maintain the interest in a 'solo' bass playing album, but of course you might think differently.

Joni Mitchell

MINGUS (1979)

*Though popularly regarded as a barbaric art,
it is to its sophistication that jazz owes its real force.
It is the first dance music to bridge the gap
between highbrow and lowbrow successfully.*
                                    Constant Lambert (1905-1951)

Charles Mingus the great jazz bassman was suffering from Lou Gehrig's disease. He contacted Joni and asked if she would consider writing some music and lyrics for a version of T.S.Eliot's 'Four Quartets' that he had wanted to create but his sickness had prevented him. He was already confined to a wheel-chair when Joni met him to discuss the project during April 1978. Lou Gehrig's disease is similar in many ways to multiple sclerosis. Joni declined the T.S.Eliot idea but she did agree to write some melodies for the six sets of lyrics that Charles had created. Joni was living in her New York apartment in the Regency Hotel. The tunes that Charles created were titled in the Anthony Braxton manner, that is Joni I to VI, just numerical.

Some conversation with Mingus was taped and used on the album. Charles Mingus was becoming a forgotten man and wanted to raise his celebrity a little before he died, he knew that his time was short. Sadly Charles Mingus died on January 5th 1979 at the age of 56, in Cuenavaca, Mexico. He never heard Joni's completed album.

MINGUS (released July 1979)

The cover was manufactured in the same design that was used on 'For the Roses' complete with the extra inner flap. The front cover painting from Joni is titled 'Sweet Sucker Dance (Abundance and Decline)' and is another of Joni's surrealistic expressionist designs. The picture shows two figures sitting on a bed, the headboard can be seen behind the head of the figure on the left, this is probably Joni herself, her hair is billowing away to the left. The other figure maybe Mingus but it does seem to be a little thin in shape to be him. Whoever it is he is playing a flute or perhaps holding something in front of his mouth. I have guessed that this is a man because in the genital region there seems to be a penis. I maybe miles from the truth but to be fair the painting should have been swapped with the painting on the rear of the cover. This depicts Charles Mingus sitting in his wheel chair, his back towards the artist, wearing a large mexican hat. Joni has not got the wheels aligned properly and the shadows seem wrong but it is more pertinent than the cover. The Mingus portrait is titled 'Chair in the Sky' which assumes that Mingus went to

Heaven. The painting shows Mingus' fingers as being like huge swollen sausages, and this is a man who made his career out of his dextrous fingers coupled with his larger than life charisma. There is a second painting of Charles this time titled 'I's a Muggin', he is smiling and looking to his left where Joni smiles down at him. The rest of the cover contains the lyrics and the 'raps' the jazzy word for conversation. The cover notes also throw up another ambivalence, were the musicians detailed on the cover actually playing on the record? The Guinness Book of Rock Stars states 'Mingus using jazz musicians Gerry Mulligan, John McLaughlin, Jan Hammer and Stanley Clarke is released'. True these musicians plus Eddie Gomez, John Guerin, Phil Woods, Tony Williams are name checked in the cover but Joni writes 'During these experimental recording dates, I had the opportunity to play with some great musicians. I would like to thank them here they helped me to search'. None of these players are detailed in the musicians list on the end of the lyrics and no permissions are requested for their inclusion. Stanley Clarke (his name is spelled wrongly on the cover) of course has always admitted that he was influenced by Mingus, but I don't believe he is playing on the album, it is Jaco Pastorius throughout. The piano is Herbie Hancock, the saxophone Wayne Shorter, with the Don Alias, Pete Erskine and Emil Richards on drums. There is one extra credit 'Wolves', we had no way of knowing at the time that Joni was approaching her lycanthropic stage, dogs and wolves would appear on later albums.

HAPPY BIRTHDAY 1975 (RAP): Is the first of the five conversational pieces on the album. Happy birthday to Charles Mingus on his 53rd birthday, born 1922.

GOD MUST BE A BOOGIE MAN: This lyric is created as a summary of the first pages of Charles' biography 'Beneath the Underdog'. An 'underdog' is a man who watches and waits, the man that attacks when he is afraid, just like canines. In the book Charles states that there might not be a God, people go to church out of fear. The church says "Come here for forgiveness, but don't change your ways or you will not need us!" The people are expected to remain poor, drunk and ragged because the church needs them to be stupid. Their country also needs them that way so that they can fight their wars for the God that they constantly remind you exists. In the lyric Joni attacks the subject from an alternative direction, men get betrayed in the divine plan. She sings 'blind rage to kill, blind faith to care'. The decision of both Joni and Charles is that 'man' is just trying to find out about himself. The band echo the title of the song at the end of each verse, except in the second verse where they sing 'bogie man', the man who will come and catch errant children in the night. Mingus according to Joni wanted to evaluate his own personal position in God's divine plan, perhaps his religion was the reason that one of his last great albums was 'Let My Children Hear Music'.

FUNERAL (RAP): The conversation with Charles continues...he says that he intends to be buried in India, his service was to be by The Vedanta Society Church, he had it already planned...... after he died Mingus was cremated.

A CHAIR IN THE SKY: The idea for this is not directly that of Charles Mingus, it is really belongs to Eldridge Cleaver, taken from his book containing his personal panacea for curing all race problems 'Soul on Ice'. Charles had hopes of being even a bigger star in his afterlife. The track opens with rain just like on the track 'Paprika Plains' on the previous album. Charles in his wheelchair, a chair that looks out over dreams of Manhattan, Birdland, Bird, running out of time. He continues in his dream of immortality, Joni said that his ego wanted to raise his credentials so that he would be remembered and revered. If this tune was written by Mingus then Joni must have found difficulty in placing the words, it was more likely just a Mingus notion taken to fruition by Joni.

THE WOLF THAT LIVES IN LINDSEY: This track and the opener are the two Joni wrote alone, Charles Mingus is given co-credit on all the others. This is the start of Joni's lycanthropic stage, she would continue it on a later album. A better title for this would have been 'It Comes and Goes'. Don Alias on congas, Joni on guitar, wolf noises to introduce us to the dereliction of the down-and-outs and the ladies of the night. I have not been able to ascertain just who 'Wolf' is supposed to be, he gets away with murder, he beats the laws of man. There have very been few cases of wolves attacking humans through history, unless they were attacked first, or the person was showing extreme fear. I did not recognise any 'wolf' character from 'Beneath the Underdog' either, perhaps it is just a fictional tale for a despairing society. Superb wolf-running scene at the coda played by Joni and Don Alias.

I'S A MUGGIN' (RAP): is the sum total of this track. A mug is slang for a fool, a face, also it can be a drinking vessel or a method of robbery......?

SWEET SUCKER DANCE: In 'Beneath the Underdog' one of the most harrowing episodes is Charles' stay in Bell Vue Mental Hospital. Charles had decided that he needed help and voluntarily walked into the hospital. He had decided that if he did not receive attention he would die. Once ensconced in a hospital full of weird patients he found that he could not just ask for a discharge and release himself; he was 'imprisoned' for treatment. One of the patients danced everywhere, light on his feet, but doomed to stay there forever. Charles survived, some of the others became broken individuals. Joni's has written one of her most under-rated lyrics for this song. Just listen again with the knowledge of this dance of insecurity and isolation, where the shadows have the saddest things to say. Charles also wrote one of his most renowned tunes whilst at Bell Vue, it was titled 'Wednesday Night Prayer Meeting'. He composed it in his head, he said it aided his recovery, but Charles was never mentally sick, why he walked into a mental hospital has never been answered. This dance of insecurity becomes a jazz song of romance, embraces and dismissals. Mingus was a survivor, others were less fortunate.

COIN IN THE POCKET (RAP): This is not titled in the gatefold just on the rear of the cover. Charles explaining that he always had the Midas touch, born lucky, always had a few dollars in his pocket. In the previous song Joni had written that Charles was 'blessed'.

THE DRY CLEANER FROM DES MOINES: This is almost 'Twisted-revisited'. After being told that he was lucky, the man from Des Moines was lucky at gambling. Slot machines, he cleaned out the machines, dry-cleaned-out the machines. He got three oranges, cherries, plums and lemons so often that watchers lost their taste for fruit. I thought three lemons lost! He won at the circus, at the card and craps tables, he was so lucky that he could put a coin into the slot of a toilet door and get '21'. Jaco Pastorius is brilliant on this track (as usual), he adds emphasis to the coda as Joni repeats 'Lucky'.

LUCKY (RAP): Charles continues to explain that he was lucky, blessed by God. He seems to have little animosity for God putting him a wheel chair due to Lou Gehrig's disease.

GOODBYE PORK PIE HAT: This song was not written about Charles although he often wore a pork pie shaped hat. This concerns The Prez, the President, Lester Young. Lester a black man who in the 1940s and 1950s travelled with a white woman companion, it was just asking for trouble in southern America. Young was arguably the greatest tenor saxophone player of the century. He played in the great Count Basie Bands. He was named The Prez by Billie Holiday, in return he named her 'Lady Day'. He was broken by the U.S. Army, he was put in a racist stockade and given a dishonourable discharge, a man who had never done anything dishonourable in his life. I remember owning a Basie Live album where Lester played a guest spot, he played the whole song in a different key signature to that of the band, and it still sounded wonderful. Lester Young refused to accept the underdog position, for him the sidewalk became a history book. It is not universally known that Lester Young started his musical career as a drummer, he only changed instrument because he was tired of setting up and taking his drum kit down. He observed the clarinet player snapping his instrument in half putting in a case and walking off with a beautiful woman, Lester spent an hour dismantling and by then all the girls had gone, he sold the drums and bought a saxophone. Joni never sounded more like Billie Holiday than she does on this track.

Joni had an extremely weird experience, or coincidence concerning this track and Charles Mingus after he had died. Joni and Don Alias were travelling on the underground when they accidentally got off the train two stations early. They saw a crowd of people applauding and shouting. In the centre of the crowd were two black boys doing the robotic-dance used by Michael Jackson in his act. They were dancing to the music coming from the jukebox inside the restaurant. Joni noticed that the club had pictures of Lester Young on the windows, when she looked up she noticed that the place was called 'The Pork Pie Hat'. Joni felt that this experience was reflected in her song of the same name, Lester the past generation, the two dancing boys the present.

The album made it to No 24 in the U.K. and No 17 in U.S.A. Joni formed a band and went on tour. She also found herself sued by The California State Equalisation Board for unpaid taxes. This case was brought against her and the musicians that had played in her bands and on recordings over the period from 1972 to 1976. The C.S.E.B. claimed an extra 15% of their earnings. The information from the courts is difficult to obtain so my information comes from newspapers at the time. Apparently the payments to the musicians were separate yet they were part of the whole recording and playing process so they had to share in the profits of those recordings and shows, and thus pay tax on those profits. I know that this sounds confusing but the C.S.E.B. had enormous government resources and showed no mercy in their search for extra taxable funds. As with all these claims if funds are available with the person or company under investigation they have to pay the surcharge requested and then go to court to fight for reimbursement. The identical situation happens in the Limited Liability companies in the U.K., if the Inland Revenue sends you a demand to pay within any time scale that 'they' decide you pay it or they may suspend your company from all trading. Joni's management paid up and she then had to spend money to fight the case. She won and the money was eventually returned, it took Joni's team ten years. In the U.K. if the money is won back then compound interest is paid in that reimbursement but it is unlikely that it would cover the cost of the litigation.

Her tour of the USA included her best band ever, they complimented her music perfectly. The band included Jaco Pastorius, Pat Metheny, Lyle Mays, Michael Brecker, The Persuasions and of course Don Alias, they played some extremely complex arrangements, perfectly. Joni and this band would record some shows in preparation for the release of Joni's second live album as a follow up to 'Miles of Aisles'.

Don Alias, Russ Kunkel and Joni recorded a track 'Nexus' with Dan Fogelberg. The song was used to open Fogelberg's 'The Innocent Age' song cycle double album, released in 1981. Joni can be heard soaring above the vocals singing descant. When I played the track, a visitor to my home was sure that the descant was actually being sung by Graham Nash, perhaps that is where Joni took her inspiration for this performance.

To return to Charles Mingus and his book 'Beneath the Underdog'. The book is of course Charles' autobiography but he did preface the book with the words 'Some names in this work have been changed and some of the characters and incidents are fictitious'. This left the reader in a dilemma as the narrative unfolds. The book (in my opinion) is a masterpiece, however if the writer had been an unknown it would most likely failed to find a publisher. It is brilliantly, although incorrectly, written in the first person, third person, as viewed by a parent, as seen by an unknown narrator and sometimes all four on the same page. The reader has to 'tune-in' to the style and the result is extremely rewarding. If one was expecting tales of jazz bands and musicians then forget it, he does of course mention them, however stories are of relationships with his parents and a multitude of readily available women. Charles repeatedly reminds us how large his penis is, it occurs so often the reader is left wondering if perhaps his description is just hyperbole and wishful thinking. The book also has a continuing love story running through it, she is Lee Marie the childhood sweetheart that became the love of his life.

Charles also presents his fastidious feelings towards God and death. On Joni's album he can be heard saying after 'God Must Be a Boogie man' "I'm gonna be buried man, I got my shit all figured out!" The following day after he died, January 5th, 1979, aged 56, in Mexico, he was cremated. When asked if he believed in God, Charles answered "yes, as a boogie man!" The predominant influence in Charles' musical-youth (according to his book) was Fats Navarro the jazz trumpeter; Charles played alongside him, Fats died at the age of 27 in 1950 of heroin addiction and tuberculosis complications. Charles also studied bass with Red Callender a player who left us very few recordings. Charles also rehearsed with Blind pianist Art Tatum the idea was for them to go on the road together as a duo, they could not find work so Tatum went out alone, he became the most dextrous, influential and accomplished pianist in jazz, ever.

Of course Charles had a larger than life ego, he even called himself Baron Mingus for a while countermanding Count Basie and Duke Ellington. He did not like to be called Charlie, but often refers to himself as that in the book, also many of his friends seemed to say 'Minkus' rather than Mingus. Just like reading books by Jack Kerouac it is necessary to attempt to put the real names to the pseudonyms used, for instance 'Red Hair' is probably Red Norvo, the rest are for you to work out. Mingus became well known for his composition 'Pithecanthropus Erectus' which is available on many compact discs. Charles Mingus was such a powerful figure in his heyday that after his death his band continued to play his music to packed nightclubs, they called themselves The Mingus Dynasty.

JONI MITCHELL

SHADOWS AND LIGHT (1980)
WILD THINGS RUN FAST (1982)

> *Music should give to poetry what the brightness of colour and the happy combination of light and shade give to a well-executed and finely composed drawing, it should fill its characters with life without destroying the outline.*
> *Christoph Willibald von Gluck (1714-1987)*

Joni's successful tour with the 'jazz' band was recorded, it was to be a double album.

SHADOWS AND LIGHT (released September 1980)

The cover photograph has Joni's face merged with a cymbal and drum and the forehead and nose of Don Alias. There are more of these double exposures which although they may be extremely 'arty' are, in my opinion, a waste of space. They are not specially clever nor are they at all interesting. We also get some stills, again taken (all double exposures) from the video of the show, a car with a boot hanging out, Jaco playing, a wolf, the band etc. There is one superb picture of Joni which is not totally spoiled by the 'photo-artist', still looking beautiful at 37. Joni claims responsibility for these photo-images she really should have known better they are a dreadful extravagance and add nothing to the packaging.

The double album (compact disc) remains one of my all-time favourite live sets. On the first compact disc release, three tracks from the vinyl set did not make it namely 'Black Crow/Don's Solo/Free Man in Paris', however they were reinstated on the re-mixed version. Those tracks are the poorest and Don Alias' drum solo (like all drum solos) is only good for listening maybe twice. The sound is so good one marvels that these tracks were actually recorded life.

INTRODUCTION: This includes a scene from James Dean's film 'Rebel Without a Cause' there is also an excerpt from Frankie Lyman and the Teenagers singing 'I'm Not a Juvenile Delinquent'. IN FRANCE THEY KISS ON MAIN STREET follows superbly mixed, Pat Metheny is the perfect foil for Jaco's bass. On EDITH AND THE KINGPIN the band threatens to overwhelm Joni, but just as it seems inevitable she holds them off. COYOTE is sung in a deep voice, she is trying to take the part of the man, the coyote. The marvellous band has improved immensely on the original studio version.

GOODBYE PORK PIE HAT has lots of arpeggios, I think Joni sings 'Don I look Up', (for Don Alias) instead of 'Don't I', Michael Brecker's tenor saxophone is upfront here. DRY CLEANER FROM DES MOINES does not improve the studio version but Jaco's bass lines are worth listening to separately. Joni is singing improvised jazz as she takes her vocal lines from Brecker's saxophone ideas.

AMELIA is sung sadly, the original was more emancipating and more celebrating. PAT'S SOLO is a soaring electric guitar solo, Joni can be heard strumming her chords to add emphasis. Pat Metheny moves from one idea to another, Lyle Mays on keyboards makes the overall sound similar to the group Tangerine Dream on amphetamines.

In HEJIRA Joni modifies the lyric to say 'strains of Michael Brecker coming through the trees', this introduces his alto saxophone solo. The album just gets better and better. BLACK CROW is driven by Don Alias with some inspired drumming, Joni sounds a little uncomfortable with the pace at times, the band doesn't miss a note. DON'S SOLO, is the expected live-show drum solo. The mixing spreads Don's arms as wide as your speakers are separated, one bongo in each. It is quite extraordinary on headphones as the drums move about. Heard twice this becomes the reason for the fast forward activator, however it is excellent for a stereo balance check. Don does perform the slow-to-fast routine which eventually segues into....DREAMLAND which becomes ethnic music, sung to assorted percussion. As the Persuasions were close by an a-cappella version would have been wonderful. FREE MAN IN PARIS opens with the band sounding like 'Weather Report'. I find it impossible not to tap my feet to this track.

BAND INTRODUCTIONS by Joni, Joni makes sure that we know that the new paramours name is Alias, al-eye-us not a-lee-us. Was (not was) had the same trouble, their name is pronounced 'w-has' not 'wars', so now you know. FURRY SINGS THE BLUES is sung very quietly, Joni adds extra emphasis on Furry's 'I don't like you' line. WHY DO FOOLS FALL IN LOVE?, is sung with The Persuasions and it is a great rock 'n' roll performance. Mike Brecker seems to think that he has become Earl Bostic, Joni sounds just like Frankie Lyman. The band and the audience are ecstatic at the performance of the song. SHADOWS AND LIGHT is a new song. The band plays a keyboard based 'Twilight Zone' introduction, and Joni follows singing in her best Joan Baez voice. The lyric is a condemnation of the selfishness of governments, and particularly the law makers. The proselytizing continues accompanied by Lyle Mays on church organ. She alters some of the lyrics 'keeper of the laws' becomes 'man of laws', that exonerate the women. Wrong or right, shadows and light, clearly not 'darkness', sometimes blindness and sight. GOD MUST BE A BOOGIE MAN is taken from a cassette recording direct from the P.A. mixer, the sound is different, but reasonable. Jaco plays the melody and the audience responds by shouting out the title line. Joni is continuing with her Annie Ross style, perhaps she should have found her own Lambert and Hendricks for the live shows. WOODSTOCK is sung differently to her original, listening to the softer more melodic versions must have changed Joni's idea of how it should sound, this is Joni's definitive version.

There were some enthusiastic reviews, this was unusual for a live album which was a re-run of previous released songs. Paul Keers wrote... 'Her voice twists and turns like silk in the wind, moving gracefully over the aggressive choppy rhythms of her band and her music, reminiscent of both Charlie Mingus and Weather Report'. Keers continued.... 'The music she composes is now as important as her stunning voice and marvellous lyrics, and as jazz is meant to be played live, it is on this double album that you can really appreciate the success and sophistication of those recent compositions'. I think Paul Keers liked it!

The album did not do as well as it deserved, it achieved No 63 in U.K. and 38 in U.S.A. The 'Shadows and Light Special' was shown on the 'Show-time' Television channel in the U.S.A. which increased the sales. I am assured that the video of the show is excellent but I have been unable to locate a copy in the European PAL system, the sound could not be an improvement to the re-mixed compact discs.

Joni appeared at the Bread and Roses Festival of Acoustic Music, at the Greek Theatre U.C. Berkeley. She went on stage and jammed for a while with Albert King. The festival included such luminaries as Joan Baez, Mimi Farina, Dave Van Ronk, Pete Seeger, Ramblin' Jack Elliott, Arlo Guthrie, The Persuasions, Richie Havens, Buffy Sainte-Marie, Country Joe McDonald, Jackson Browne and more. Joni and Albert's session was not included on the album release, nor are they on the Big Beat Records compact disc, which includes all the others mentioned above. On the inner gatefold of the vinyl double album there is a photograph of Bob Dylan with the inference that he is there on the record somewhere, if he is then I can't hear him.

On February 5th 1981 Joni was inducted by Canadian President, Pierre Trudeau, into Canada's Juno Hall of Fame. Joni had a quiet year in 1982 and during this time the relationship with Don Alias ended, the new man in her life was the much younger (by 13 years) Larry Klein, a bass player. It seemed that Joni only liked acoustic instrument musicians, Chuck Mitchell, David Crosby, Graham Nash, James Taylor, John Guerin, Don Alias and now Larry Klein. As she had moved away from drummers to Larry Klein I was immediately reminded of the old musician's joke concerning rhythm sections, and I hope you will excuse me for including it here, it does seem relevant.

It goes..A musician was on tour in darkest Africa for the first time. When he woke up one morning he could hear drumming coming from the far off hills. He asked the concierge what was the drumming for?

He said "Master if the drums stop a terrible thing will happen".

The musician attempted to find out just how bad it would be if the drums stopped but could get no further information. He finally found another African musician and asked him what the terrible thing would be if the drumming stops.

He looked furtively around and whispered...

"Master if the drumming stops then a terrible thing happens...a bass solo!"

So now Joni was with her bass player Larry Klein, as Don Alias got a drum solo on 'Shadows and Light' could we now expect bass solos on Joni's records. Joni also decided to change record labels again. This time she signed with David Geffen's 'Geffen Records', she also parted with manager Elliot Roberts as her manager after 17 years. As a replacement she settled on Peter Asher as manager of her business affairs. Asher was part of The Peter and Gordon duo in the sixties and started his management of musicians with James Taylor in Taylor's Apple Records days.

WILD THINGS RUN FAST (released November 1982)

Joni decided to make a rock 'n' roll album, she had moved away from jazz with this release. The cover was another Joni Mitchell painting. She is standing and leaning on a television on which the picture is of wild horses running fast. I mentioned that the Mingus cover had strange perspectives, here the floor is wrong, the table is falling over. The pair of ladies shoes should be on the floor but when open the gatefold out they seem to be much higher off the floor, the carpet is hovering above the skirting board under the shoes. This of course may be all intentional, Joni's self portrait is however excellent. We have three more paintings on the inside, a pair of wild white horses, Joni leaning back in a loving embrace with Larry Klein and a chair which has an art book open at the Matisse painting of 'The Dance (1910)', the chair appears to be standing on an unfinished painting and we get a plan view of brushes in a vase. One wonders why the Matisse painting included was not 'The Music' which is in exactly the same style and painted at the same time, it shows figures sitting listening to a piper play, far more relevant to Joni's music.

Looking through the musicians on the album one notices the total absence of Don Alias (except for assisting in the arranging of 'Be Cool'), David Guerin returns on four tracks, the other drumming is supplied by Frank Zappa's superb drummer Vinnie Colaiuta. Pat Metheny and Jaco Pastorius have moved on and Steve Lukather and Larry Klein replace them, Wayne Shorter returns and James Taylor, Lionel Richie assists on backing vocals.

CHINESE CAFE: On 'Song for Sharon' Joni wrote the lyric as though it was a letter to a friend, here she does the same, the confidant this time is 'Carol', a friend from the old days that now has children. Joni mentions her own child born to her but not raised by her. The land has been taken from the Red Indians for exploration for uranium. These days at The Chinese Cafe were back in 1955, the song on the juke-box at the time was 'Unchained Melody', the melody from the film 'Unchained', of course. The dreams of two girls only seem a few years ago, where does the time go? Joni has cleverly interrupted the end of each verse with a line from 'Unchained Melody', it only takes the song over at the end when the two girls sit in the Chinese Cafe dreaming about the future. Strange thing concerning the 'Unchained melody' is that everyone remembers the song but hardly anyone remembers the film.

WILD THINGS RUN FAST: Joni impersonates Reg Presley; as I sit writing this Reg Presley lives less then 100 metres from here yet I have never seen him in the flesh. An up-tempo song with a heavier sound, this is Joni's version of Shakespeare's 'Taming of the Shrew', viewed from the feminist's point of view. The female of the species is the predator, she thought she had him tamed. He has left in a hurry and she thought that he loved her. It has been mooted that this song concerns drugs and departing for another woman, well to me that appears to be someone searching for problems within a quite innocuous love-lost lyric.

LADIES MAN: This must be a song to Larry Klein, she was won over by him with just a glance, love at first sight. At least here she is aware that he is likely to be a heartbreaker. The vacillation, the trepidation, he is he worth taking a chance on. This song could be a man used as a metaphor for some heartbreaking-cocaine, it could wreck anybody's dream.

MOON AT THE WINDOW: Joni mentions the faucet once again as she did on 'Marcie', Harry Nilsson used it on 'Think About Your Troubles' in his pop filmed cartoon musical, narrated by Dustin Hoffman, 'The Point'. A jazz song in Joni's favourite Annie Ross style. Drug and drink references again, in spoon and glass, although Joni has loved and lost so many times, she has become hardened, the moon continues to mean romance. The lovers (or the drugs) have stolen everything except the Moon.

SOLID LOVE: This is probably Joni's deepest surrendering to love in a song. Real happiness and trust, he is everything, love on a firm foundation, solid love, you open my heart. A beautiful ballad of love for the man she loves, this could be represented in the painting on the top right hand corner of the inner gatefold, happiness at last.

BE COOL: Advice to lovers who find themselves in the pain of separation. Whether this 'play it cool' counselling is suitable for all is the question. What must be said is that after the affairs were over for Joni she managed to remain on extremely close terms with her ex-paramours. The inference seems to be just let them go, don't show any emotion, smile and don't whine. In all relationships the partner that loves least will always have the upper-hand in the partnership, of that there is no doubt. Here Joni has decided that there is a 50 percent chance of ex-lovers returning if you play it cool. This song segues into....

.....(YOU'RE SO SQUARE) BABY I DON'T CARE : The Lieber and Stoller song written for Elvis Presley for his 'Jailhouse Rock' film in 1957. I'm not sure if Joni meant this as her version of 'how to keep cool', the song denigrates the man's attitudes but does not reduce her love for him, it is she that 'don't care'. Joni certainly enjoys singing the song, Vinnie Colaiuta on drums and Larry Klein on bass drive the song along, with Larry Williams and Kim Hutchcroft adding the brass segments. This is arguably the best ever version by a female, in fact I think it is the only version by a female singer.

YOU DREAM FLAT TIRES: A bounce-beat rocker, Lionel Richie adds some vocals, a song of love and re-assurance. So love can be repaired as easy as flat tyres can be replaced? The narrator really wants more than just a flirtation she needs it all to be more permanent.

MAN TO MAN: The backing band is more like a lover's score sheet, James Taylor, John Guerin, Larry Klein. With these ex-lovers in tow Joni is singing of her own promiscuity, moving from man to man. One can imagine her looking and smiling at each of these men in turn as she sings. Joni exorcises a few more of her ghosts here. A lot of good guys have come through her 'door', is that metaphorically? A brave lyric especially knowing what reaction was likely from The Rolling Stone Magazine.

UNDERNEATH THE STREET LIGHT: These lyrics are similar to what Tom Waits was writing at the time. Joni professing her love, no, she is swearing her love for Larry Klein. Joni swears on all the surrounding people and things within her panoramic vision.

LOVE: Love is the greatest beauty. The first mistake is that the cover states that the lyric is drawn from The Bible, Corinthians II:13, it is not, it comes from Corinthians I:13. 'Although I speak in tongues of men and angels' and 'the gift of prophecy' are the basic tenets of the song. The Book of Corinthians Chapter 14 is full of 'tongues' , Chapters 12/13/14 packed full of 'gifts'. Joni adds 'rejoices in the truth' which is prefixed by 'rejoice not in iniquity' which is from Corinthians I Chapter 13. Bob Dylan used tracts from The Book of Isaiah un-credited in his songs, here Joni gives the credit but the wrong Biblical Book, it might have been a ploy to get writers like me searching through their respective Concordances.

Joni and Larry Klein married on 21st November 1982, in Malibu, California. The 'Wild Things Run Fast' album reached No 25 in U.S.A. and 32 in U.K. 'Baby I Don't Care' taken from the album and released as a single only got as high as No 47 in USA.

DOG EAT DOG (1985)
CHALK MARK IN A RAINSTORM (1988)

I am saddest when I sing, so are those who hear me,
they are sadder even than I am.
                    Charles Farrar Browne (1834-1867)

Joni embarked on a long tour that took five months to complete. She appeared in Japan, New Zealand, Australia, then travelled on through Europe she appeared in the U.K. at Wembley in April 1983. One of the performances in Italy had a bootleg recording made which was easily available. Joni's music was changing yet again, she had gone from folk to pop to Jazz and Rock, now it was synthesized electronic music that caught her ear. Thomas Dolby had released some successful albums and she called on him to create some special arrangements for her next album. Thomas Dolby had been originally employed to add 'colour' behind Joni's voice, Joni agreed; however on the album he was actually employed (unknown to Joni) to add some 'excitement'. Joni was said to be more than a little peeved, however on listening to the album Thomas Dolby only adds 'colour'. My assumption is that Joni as the artist who would ultimately suffer the criticism had the last word on the production.

DOG EAT DOG (released October 1985)

The gradual invasion of Joni's psyche by wolves comes of age in the cover design. We had wolves on the Mingus album, the song Jericho mentions the 'dog kennelled in her', now lycanthropy arrives in the cover art. Joni has taken photographs of herself and some wolves, she constructed a collage and then painted over the photographs. To the left of the open gatefold there is a car that has been involved in an accident. Wolves are patrolling around the car. A picture of Joni snarling is set to the right hand side of the cover one wolf is looking up at her, the others are coming towards her. Joni has used paint and coloured felt tipped pens (probably) to add colour to the animals and her own hair. The darkened areas are painted in green in varying intensities. The design is effective but hardly a work of art. The two pictures on the inside, one of Joni with two wolves and an extra wolf peering in from the right hand side, have been half coloured-in. Joni has missed one of the rear legs of the red wolf, the other solo wolf seems to be chewing a cigar. The lyrics are typewritten over a grey paint wash. One wonders if this breakdown of a car and the emerging wolves is a fantasy fear, the attack by wolves on humans is considered a rarity, but like all canines they can sense fear and respond accordingly to protect themselves. There are old proverbs that state 'Dog does not eat dog but men will eat each other up like cannibals (1651 & 1869)' and 'A wolf will never make war against another wolf (1790)', it likely that the first was the influence for the album title, the inferences abound throughout the record.

Joni told Mick Brown that she had to fight the record company to get the album issued in a gatefold sleeve. As she was selling fewer 'units' than previously she also was advised to use a producer for this album. Joni's opinion of producers is not generous, she thinks that they are men that watch football games on the studio television, talk on the phone and then throw their weight about. She accepted Thomas Dolby as co-producer, but not on all the tracks. The album was to be the most expensive of all her albums so far.

The musicians used from the previous album were Larry Klein (bass), Mike Landau (guitar) and Vinnie Colaiuta (drums), to these were added Michael Fisher (percussion/samples) and of course Thomas Dolby who played keyboards and did the arrangements for the synthesizers. Two of the songs were Klein/Mitchell compositions, all the remainder by Joni. Ex-Doobie Brother Michael McDonald, ex-Eagle Don Henley, ex-paramour James Taylor, plus Wayne Shorter also augment some of the tracks. Rod Steiger also acts the part of a crazed evangelist on 'Tax Free'. Klein/Mitchell/Dolby and Mike Shipley are all credited as Producers.

GOOD FRIENDS: Michael McDonald the ex-Doobie Brother sings on this track. McDonald also spent some time with Steely Dan. He seems to have perfected the singing duet. He had a minor hit with Nicolette Larson in 1980, and a No 4 hit in 1983 singing solo on 'Keep Forgettin'. He went Top 20 with James Ingram in 1984, and the following year after recording with Joni (1986), he had a No 1 with Patti Labelle with the contradictory titled 'On my Own'. The script of the 'Good Friends' lyric reminds me of 'Beautiful Friendship', two friends that may become two lovers and this possibly will spoil everything. Unscrupulous clandestine meetings, two friends who meet when their other relationship has encountered problems. Thomas Dolby adds his electronic wizardry to the backing. As a duet there are marked similarities with 'Up Where We Belong' the theme from the film 'An Officer and a Gentleman', a duet sung by Jennifer Warnes and Joe Cocker it reached No 1 in October 1982.

FICTION: Perhaps Greig should have been credited with some of the melody, it follows Peer Gynt in places. Thomas Dolby has created a selection of drums and gizmo effects as a backing, Joni, Larry Klein, Joe Smith and Thomas

Dolby add the voices. The fiction of life created by advertising, obscuring the truth, creating desires, taking our money. Joni has created her list of elusive dreams of the buy me, watch me, listen to me image-makers. It is all a fiction, all plastic, there is a bizarre thought to add. In my opinion most people realise that it is all a fiction but like to led along, they are pleased to be associated with their favourite people, the curious fact is without all of them the rest of us could manage perfectly, that is except for the hangers-on. What we have to think after this song is finished is that perhaps Joni's moralising advice on the song is also part of 'the fiction'.

THE THREE GREAT STIMULANTS: Thomas Dolby's electronic accompaniment must owe some dues to the work of Laurie Anderson here. Joni continues with her moralising themes, this time it is the futility of war. The U.S.A. is lucky that throughout its short history it has never been invaded, and apart from Pearl Harbour way out in The Pacific Ocean, has not been bombed from the air. The three great stimulants in Joni's song are 'artifice', 'brutality' and 'innocence'. So the incentives are.. a crafty or subtle deception -cruelty-untainted by corruption. Bombs continue to be made by 'madmen', and in the final verse Joni changes tack to present a metaphorical prophecy that these trouble times will change the hearts of all mankind, to that I answer..perhaps. I wonder why Joni refers to 'madmen' and not 'mad-women', think of all the women Presidents and Prime Ministers and then try to think of one that has not had a war or serious unrest to contend with, difficult isn't it..Ireland, Israel, Pakistan, France, Great Britain......etc.

TAX FREE: Corresponding to the feelings of Frank Zappa, Joni turns her attention towards the hellfire evangelists, Jimmy Swaggart probably. One major problem for other working people is that religions do not have to pay taxes. Joni was suddenly made aware of her tax problems, and I assume it is the same in the U.S.A. as the U.K., if the Inland Revenue make a claim against you then you pay first then present arguments to get it back. Rod Steiger acts the role of the evangelist on the track. In an interview with Mick Brown, Joni stated 'they (tax people) are slamming my industry'. She continued.... 'there was a time when rock 'n' roll could fill the same stadiums as these evangelists, and in some ways get more respect. I think there is an envy there because it is all show-business'. As the evangelists take time on television advertising their 'wares' surely they should be considered part of that entertainment industry, especially as so many so called 'Prophets of God' have been proven to be charlatans. Frank Zappa wanted to know just what the donations were for, they have a 24 hour gospel channel on television because it became so lucrative. The crooked christians have their own private Heaven on Earth. I would like to point out that an evangelist is described in my dictionary as 'an occasional preacher, sometimes itinerant'.

Joni adds her favourite expletive to the lyrics and this time it did not suffer the from the censor's pen. She writes 'When the church and State hold hands, Fuck it, I'm going dancing', a sentiment of which I whole-heartedly agree; a great lyric, should be on the national curriculum. Not only do they preach love they preach hate against Castro, Khomeini and Kaddafi, all in the name of God, and of course the attacked retaliate by invoking their own personal God, who of course will be on their side. The album is worth the price of admission just for this track, Joni's most powerful statement ever.

SMOKIN'(Empty Try Another): The accompaniment is provided by a cigarette, the craving for nicotine, no more no less.

DOG EAT DOG: A song that suggest the workers, the slaves and the genuine people will be cast aside by the rich. Joni continues to harangue the evangelists on he television screen, but now she adds the racketeers and the lawyers touting for work. The flim-flam-man makes an appearance he was the object of a great song by Laura Nyro on her 'First Songs' album. In this dog-eat-dog society when all morals are at an all-time low, Joni seems to be living in newly married bliss watching television and getting agitated by what she sees. A great song, the more money you have the better justice it can buy!

SHINY TOYS: Thomas Dolby provides electronic backing clap-claps, another excellent up-tempo song. The possessions that success can buy, a Porsche, a beagle and a toupee. Joni is reading a magazine in the supermarket check-out lane, perhaps she is beginning to suffer from an overdose of domesticity. A song of observing people and things around her, she has done this many times before, it is part of the writer's art.

ETHIOPIA: More television pictures that went around the world, the famine in Ethiopia that followed their war with Somalia. This must have been an extremely difficult song to play, Wayne Shorter is following some unusual chords even for Joni. My original thought was that she had tuned her guitar incorrectly, whatever happened it is most arresting. Joni has switched the objective from The Horn of Africa to Brazil (I think) and the deforestation, there was not much forest in Ethiopia. I thought that Joni was going to move on to the fact that we in the West cared for these poor people in Africa, but their own selfish governments cared not one jot. As Joni has such inherent bile for the television churches one wonders why she did not also point an angry finger at the tax-free charities that spend more money on their own private bureaucracy than the needy people for whom the money is intended in the first place.

IMPOSSIBLE DREAMER: Wayne Shorter is only present on this track (and the next), perhaps he was working away, he seemed to be part of the Joni entourage. A lovely and gentle song on which Alex Acuna plays 'Bata' whatever that is. As an opposite to the previous track Joni is now thinking of the land of plenty, the land of the free. Joni sits in her lonely room thinking of her man, hoping he is returning the compliment. Is peace between two lovers impossible?

LUCKY GIRL: This could be an answer record for Kylie Minogue's 'I Should Be So Lucky', Joni has luckily met Larry Klein. A great song for Joni once again besotted by the man in her life, but this time more so, she decided to actually marry the man, for life! Joni realises that she has been all over the World, her mission impossible, (probably a reference to the previous track), is over at last. Before she would only trust a man as far as she could throw her shoe. The track ends Joni's most moralising album ever, she sounds at times like an agony-aunt answering her own questions. This is yet another album that improves with repeated playing, sounds as good now as ever, the advice was not taken, as more than ten years later all the problems to which Joni refers are still in place, and still continue to cause pain. An album that stimulates the thoughts of the listener. Joni's had a growing dislike of the changes in America from liberal law making to a far right-wing stance that made the population feel powerless. The album delicately and cunningly attacks ecological inconsideration and big business, both combine to create moral decay in religious standards.

The critics were extremely unkind to the album, they considered it even worse than its predecessor and they slaughtered that. David Geffen was known to be a business man first a music lover sixth or lower. The album reached only No 63 in U.S.A. and 57 in the U.K., this is 30 places lower than 'Wild Things Run Fast', Joni's appeal was dwindling, and fast. The records were costing a fortune to make and not making adequate returns for the Geffen Label. The albums were dropped from the lists in 1989, then reinstated as an 'Integrity product'. Joni went on the U.K. talk show 'Wogan' (March 1986) to promote the album, this was followed by an appearance on The B.B.C. 2 late night programme The Old Grey Whistle Test (April 1986). She told Richard Skinner that she was leaving the music business and retiring..... after she had made three more albums!

Joni appeared at The Meadowlands Festival in New Jersey. She was giving her time free for the aid of Amnesty International. As she was singing missiles were thrown onto the stage by the unappreciative audience. It is more likely that these imbeciles had been pelting all the acts not just Joni. Police (the group) and U2 who were also on the bill and were also treated like baseball receivers. She sang the song 'The Three Great Stimulants' which has a sort of stream of consciousness lyric from 'Dog Eat Dog', and 'Number One' which was a new composition which would be recorded for the next album (Chalk Mark).

The track 'Good Friends' was released as a single but was a flop it just climbed to No 85 in Billboard's listing before oblivion.

David Geffen hoped for a better public response from Joni's next album. Joni and Larry produced the album and to raise the awareness level they employed some well known names with decent followings of their own. Peter Gabriel, Don Henley (again), Tom Petty, Willie Nelson, Billy Idol, Wendy and Lisa, ex-Cars bassist Benjamin Orr and Thomas Dolby once more arranging the keyboards.

CHALK MARK IN A RAIN STORM (released April 1988)

The album must have cost a fortune to make, it was recorded in nine different studios, there are only ten tracks; there are also 18 engineers credited on the sleeve. David Geffen must have been feeling very benevolent at the time. The cover was more basic than usual. The cover is credited to Glen Christensen and Joni, the photographs taken by Larry Klein. Joni wearing a wide brimmed hat has a Red Indian rug wrapped around her shoulders as she pensively looks to the right. He face is blazed with light and set against a hazy landscape of hills and trees, the sun seems to be setting behind her. The inner of the gatefold has a snake entering the lyrics from the right hand bottom corner, in the top left hand corner Joni is sleeping wrapped in the blanket. The blanket has snake-like colours and patterns, she is lying in almost the same position as the snake, one assumes that this is intentional.

MY SECRET PLACE: Manu Katche on drums and Peter Gabriel is adding vocals on this opening track, Joni is singing in a very deep and subdued voice. Most people have a secret place where they can go when all their problems seem insurmountable. We all need a refuge or sanctuary to escape from the big city life. For me the only place where hurt and anger can't encroach is within my brain, it would not surprise me to learn that Joni's secret place is identical to mine. The melody is a beguine or bossa nova, a song that is not memorable except for Joni's unusual deep vocal.

NUMBER ONE: Benjamin Orr from the group 'Cars' is present on additional vocals. This is a similar idea to Billie Holiday's 'God Bless the Child'. The desire to be one-up on the others, the need for ownership. The U.S.A. has become a place where fair-play and sportsmanship have been replaced by the necessity to be the winner, people only wish to associate with the number one. Second place might just as well have been last. The sentiments of Joni's earlier song 'Dog Eat Dog are revisited here.

LAKOTA: The track opens with a chant from a Red Indian named Iron Eyes Cody. Joni again brings to our attention the plight of the Red Indians. However I am not sure that they would agree with the line 'Sun pity me', these people are proud and courageous. Their land was being excavated for uranium and other ores, for 60 years they had been speaking to the deaf ears of the government. Lakota is an all encompassing name for the tribes that were usurped by the white man's greed, broken by the bullet and gallons of free booze. They are standing in a 'waken' manner, whatever that is, perhaps they have only just woken to the problem, a concept that seems nonsensical.

THE TEA LEAF PROPHECY (Lay Down Your Arms): The story of Joni's mother Myrtle's tea leaves has been told before. Waiting for a man during wartime the gypsy foretells the arrival of Bill, working for the military in Canada. Myrtle has subsequently said that she would be leaving her home and moving, but she never does.

DANCIN' CLOWN: This is Joni Mitchell goes disco. Frank Zappa did the same with his 'Dancing Fool'. It seems that Joni is spending her married time at home watching old movies. Jesse and Rowdy Yates are name checked here so she is watching 'Rawhide'. Rowdy Yates was played by an emerging actor named Clint Eastwood, I wonder what ever happened to him? Whenever loves come around one of the participants is always the dancing clown, in all relationships the partner that loves least will always have the upper hand. Joni's french diction needs a little attention, she sings cher-chay-la-'farm', but it may of course be intentional.

COOL WATER: Written by Bob Nolan in 1948 and first popularized by Vaughn Monroe and the Sons of the Pioneers. Frankie Laine also recorded a memorable version, of course he also recorded 'Rawhide' which connects him to the previous track. The song is now registered to Elvis Presley Music and on this version Joni duets with Willie Nelson. It is an ideal song for Willie Nelson's style but I could not locate another version of the song by him. There are versions by Frank Ifield, Tom Jones, Marty Robbins, Jack Scott, Slim Whitman and many more. I can only assume that Joni included it as part of her desire for more ecological thoughts, the version is adequate but not special.

THE BEAT OF BLACK WINGS: Joni uses the words fuckin' and piss on this song, they are uncensored on the gatefold lyrics. This is the song that included the title of the album, neatly picked out in orange type. This is the story of Killer Kyle, trained to be a soldier and sent to war. He returned almost deaf with shell-shock, he remembers that his wife aborted their child. He eases the pain by drinking booze, he earns the money for it as a pavement artist, as fast as he draws the pictures the rain washes them away. Joni brilliantly uses the word 'vicarious' in the lyric, probably the first time it has been used in song. It perfectly describes in a word the situation of the Generals at war-time. Vicarious means 'to under-go second hand participation in another's experiences', I doubt if anyone has ever put it better, sublime Mitchell!

SNAKES AND LADDERS: If there is a single on the album then this is it. Don Henley takes a fair share of the vocal and makes this repetitious but excellent song sound just like an Eagles track. Using the game of snakes and ladders as the basis Joni explains how life has its ups-and-downs. It might be love, marriage or success, as soon as you are at the bottom start climbing back up. This is similar in its idea to 'Pick Yourself Up', sell the vineyard, call the lawyer, great fun for those that participate in such shenanigans.

THE REOCCURRING DREAM: Is a return to the premise presented in 'Number One'. In this song 'Recognize this' is repeated by an un-credited male voice possibly that of Larry Klein. This dream is created by the promoters of products. The people wish to be associated with the glamorous people, the movie stars, and the products endorsed by those stars. The predominant problem is that the vast majority realise and understand the hyperbole, but like Joni they enjoy it and play along with it.

A BIRD THAT WHISTLES: Is based on the traditional song Corrina Corrina. The song is not really traditional at all, it was written in 1932 by J.Mayo Williams, and first sung by Bo Chapman, and popularised by Cab Calloway. Ray Peterson had a hit with the song in 1961. There are various spellings of the song title such as Corrine Corrina, and Corina Corina but the basic tune is similar. Dean Martin recorded an excellent version in his Dean 'Tex' Martin days, Bob Dylan sang it on 'Freewheelin', over 50 versions are registered. Joni's version is a throw-away track to complete the album, Wayne Shorter plays a birdsong coda on saxophone.

The album did better than the previous album but was not a great financial success. In the U.S.A. it reached No 45 in the U.K. No 26. In the U.K. this was the highest for her since Mingus in 1979 which had reached No 24. The critics said that Joni had included too much of the electronic effects, which had spoiled the album. In June 1989 Virgin records released a single to save the Amazonian rain forests, funds created for 'The Earth Love Fund'. I have always been perplexed just where this ecology money goes. Does it go direct to the Brazilian government so that they can have enough funds so that they need not cut down trees, does it just fund more advertising, or are there a team of itinerant tree planters following up the deforestation? Joni was one of the cast on the record with other luminaries such as Kate Bush, Bonnie Raitt, Brian Wilson, XTC, and The Ramones.

Joni Mitchell

NIGHT RIDE HOME (1991)
TURBULENT INDIGO (1994)

Night and silence-these are two of the things I cherish most.
Benjamin Britten (1913-1976)

Joni was at home painting and it was 1990 before she emerged. She took part in ex-Pink Floyd leader Roger Waters' performance of 'The Wall' which took place in Potzdamer Platz, adjacent to the Berlin Wall. The performance was relayed via satellite to television services around the world and raised money for 'The Memorial Fund for Disaster Relief'; Joni sang 'Goodbye Blue Sky'.

It was now Joni's paintings that were gaining her more popularity. She exhibited at The Broadgate Gallery, London. They had an exhibition titled 'Canada in the City' which was sub-titled 'An exhibition of Canadian Art, Music and Culture'. Joni (accompanied by Larry Klein at the exhibition) had many canvases on show, she had been on a sentimental pilgrimage in Canada with husband Larry. The result was many landscapes and portraits which had Van Gogh and Magritte influences. It seemed from her interviews at the time that the double exposure photographs on the 'Shadow and Light' cover was in fact now transferred to her painting style. Trees were in the face portrait's eyes, the road travels up her nostril, her nose is a field of wheat and Larry is standing in it. All typical surrealistic stuff, remember Joni left art school because the teachers were only interested in teaching her class in 'impressionistic surrealism'. Don Van Vliet had also ceased his music career to be an artist, however when I visited an exhibition of Don's art I found it extremely difficult to decide just who his influences are. His massive canvases are surrealistic and so are the titles, many would be suitable for his enigmatic song titles.

Joni and Don van Vliet have sold their work for massive sums, at the Broadgate Exhibition one canvas was reported to have been sold for £35,000. Back home Joni was embroiled in another embarrassment, her housekeeper sued her for assault. Joni's housekeeper (a woman) was from Guatemala. Joni told Phil Sutcliffe in an interview in 'Q' Magazine that she (Joni) had kicked the woman in the shins after an argument. Apparently the woman had been paid to travel home for a visit and used the money to go to Europe instead. The woman sued Joni for $5 million and lost. Joni was definitely becoming a winner in law, if not in love. The relationship with Larry Klein was starting to show signs of deterioration.

NIGHT RIDE HOME (released March 1991)

The cover was again the double exposure photographic design that Joni was incorporating into some of her paintings, 'Hejira', 'Shadows and Light' both had these types of pictures, Joni must have considered them part of her 'art'. Joni's face is looking towards the camera, a man (probably Larry Klein) is in silhouette chewing a small stick, maybe a matchstick, both the faces are overlaid on a lakescape or seascape with hills in the background. The rear has just the mouth and nostrils of Joni set above dark hills and trees on the horizon. Joni's lips give the impression that they are the sunset from the rear of the 'Chalk Mark' album cover. The vinyl (not compact disc) gatefold also adds Joni set against a car's wing mirror and a barn.

On this album only one composition is co-composed with husband Larry, previously he had been writing the music for Joni's lyrics. The album was recorded in Joni Mitchell's studio in her home in Bel Air, called The Kiva. One would suppose that David Geffen would want to keep his costs for Joni's albums as low as possible as her records were selling less and less.

NIGHT RIDE HOME: Like 'Hejira' Joni is back in the car observing the scene as she passes. There are crickets or electronic insects on the backing. It is the 4th of July American Independence Day, the fun and the fireworks. She is travelling with Larry Klein, she admits to being in love, a love that has endured. They are escaping the telephones and finding time to be together.

PASSION PLAY (When All the Slaves are Free): This is a crucifixion song, the killer nails set against modern days problems with the environment. Jesus was kind and redeeming, a magician and physician, perhaps Joni feels that she is a born again christian, it seems that she is aware just how far she has wandered into the wilderness. The Exxon oil disaster is the alternative theme on this superb arrangement, yet there is only a quartet of musicians.

CHEROKEE LOUISE: The Red Indians again, they seem to constantly invade the psyche of Joni. Cherokee Louise has abandoned the plains of home and lives under a railway bridge, she is running scared from her sexually abusive foster father. This is powerful, the family of Louise were always fighting, she was only happy when she was away from the home. The backing comprises of snorks and burps from Wayne Shorter on soprano saxophone and Vinnie Colaiuta's snare drum, I suspect that Joni wanted the backing to be as desolate at the lyric's scenario.

THE WINDFALL (Everything For Nothing): Joni is reflecting on her life as a star. She visits the plush stores, she has all the trappings of wealth but because she doesn't give gifts to her staff like Elvis Presley, they assume that she is mean. She believes that people are envious of her, perhaps Joni is self-creating her own star-paranoia. Gradually the lyric becomes more obvious as Joni is wagging her finger at the men that she has loved who get to share her life style for free. We then learn that she is a woman that is divorcing a gold-digger man, can this be Larry Klein, after all he is playing on this track. Whoever is the object of Joni's malice he seems to be a liar.

SLOUCHING TOWARDS BETHLEHEM: The lyric booklet explains that this track is based on the W.B.Yeats poem 'The Second Coming'. The death of organised religion and the arrival of the new Messiah. The falcon on its widening cabled arc (gyre), is a metaphor for the orbit of the World. The innocence of religion is dying, we await the new child of Bethlehem. The chimera had the head of a lion, here the head is of a man and the body of a lion. Is this Ethiopia, the lion of Ra, the drums are African influenced, the percussion superb created by Alex Acuna and Vinnie Colaiuta. It is difficult to decide to what Joni is alluding in her modification of the Yeats poem, it maybe the march of the Muslim faith, and there again it may not. The lyric is not all Yeats, Joni has added and adapted yet she gives the full lyric acknowledgement to W.B.Yeats; even the title changes Yeats' 'slouches' to 'slouching'. In her career Joni has rarely used poetry by others in her work, in her love of Yeats she is in harmony with Van Morrison. Morrison supplied a track 'Before the World was Made' to the various artists celebration of Yeats' work titled 'Now And In Time to Be'.

COME IN FROM THE COLD: Is a wonderful song, one of Joni's best for years, a sure fire hit, that is if it was released as a single and given some promotion. In the lyric Joni mentions the bonfires in her spine, this of course resulted from the polio she suffered as a child which left her with a twisted set of vertebrae. The jive dancing of 1957 when holding hands and spinning from your partner without touching was the norm. We did the 'creep' so that we could get up close, seems that in Canada they never did slow close dancing. Joni again mentions her big mistake, the pregnancy, here she calls it her 'loving crime'. As a teenager all she wanted to do was take a chance, enjoy herself, leave the confines of the area, although she did all these things it remains obvious after all these years she still has that awful guilt over becoming pregnant and giving the child up for adoption. At least in her position as a songwriter she can share the guilt, she can cudgel herself for her own misgivings. The truth is that probably only Joni considers it a necessary reason for continual chastisement. The song is a sublime seven minutes, freedom for women (and Joni) after many years of personal emancipation.

NOTHING CAN BE DONE: The only co-written song on the album, Larry Klein seems to have been taking more of a back seat in the production. This is their own personal contract for harmony. Joni worrying about her age, she is much older than husband Larry. It is repetitious but infectious, Vinnie Colaiuta is not name checked but surely it is him on drums and Alex Acuna on bongoes. David Baerwald is singing the duet vocals with Joni, perhaps Larry was already on his way out?

THE ONLY JOY IN TOWN: Latin rhythms, a song set in Spain and Rome, probably Joni is turning the pages of an art book. The Venus on a clam painting by Botticelli, Joni wants one of a Black Boy with fuschias in his hair. Joni is in Spain but keeps her distance from a beautiful boy whom she seems to be lusting after. He is so beautiful that she says in her youth she would have followed him on the first day of spring. The emancipation is complete now we have women stalking men, perhaps she just wants to paint him?

RAY'S DAD'S CADILLAC: Very similar to the jazzy style of Rickie Lee Jones, of Chuck E's In Love fame. Brenda Russell adds vocals in this duet. Joni takes us back to the rock 'n' roll days of the weekends cruisin' in the cadillac. The days of love in the back-seat, Motown music on the radio, nostalgia, remembering things better than they really were. A great song another single that never was.

TWO GREY ROOMS: This again could be a return to the early days of innocent love. A girl at home dreaming of someone she adores who is passing below her window on their way to work, they don't pass at the weekends. It might just be a phantom lover, the lonely loser in her depression and isolation pining for a lost love. Joni writes that it was 30 years ago which would be 1961, and she would have been 18 years old. The song is reminiscent of Scott Walker's 'It's Raining Today', or 'Rosemary' both songs of lonely anticipation. This final track on Joni's album is blessed with a superb orchestration from The Jeremy Lubbock Strings, it closes the album perfectly.

The reviews were good, one stated that 'Miss Mitchell never worries about surpassing her own superlative standards-she just gets up an sings'. It went on...'Her first album in three years this is the confident work of a master craftswoman marshalling her exquisite introspective melodies and soothing bird song voice, the songs say it all'. The New Musical Express thought that this album was a return to her roots, meaning hard edged acoustic guitar strums and soft vocals. They continued by writing that Joni was just a folkie again, albeit a more sophisticated one; she was never a folkie!

A video 'Come in from the Cold' was created using songs from 'Chalk Mark' and 'Night Ride'. Joni narrated and the songs were set against stills and arty colours, and as Max Bell put it 'the songs are airily beautiful, the cinematography banal, much of it looking like high grade commercials', a perfect description. Max Bell went on to write.... 'Indians and buffalo Gods in 'Lakota' does at least add a sense of purpose to the heart wrenching, stick to the album'; I agree especially with his final remark. Phil Sutcliffe wrote .... 'that there was a lot of 'monochrome, arty. chiaroscuro and not much happening'. Joni does dance around her kitchen for 'Dancing Clown', recorded in home-movie style. The blacking up for 'The Beat of Black Wings', distracts from the beauty of the song. Phil Sutcliffe concluded by writing.... 'Perhaps, by the end she'd found her video feet, but for now it's the familiar pattern of glorious music undermined by modest visual achievement'.

After twelve years of marriage Joni parted from Larry Klein, it had been by far her longest relationship ever and they had obviously brought each other much love and comfort, but no offspring. The Los Angeles riots were in progress at the time, Joni was now just a year short of her 50th birthday. The ending of the marriage also coincided with Joni going into the studio to record her next album. Peter Asher still operating as Joni's business manager moved Joni back to Mo Ostin at Warner/Reprise Records, she had been with him 23 years earlier. Joni was convinced that David Geffen hadn't sold her albums very well to the public so she decided that she wanted a change. She had considered giving her next album to Geffen as a final parting 'gift' but decided otherwise. David Geffen with his business interest brain decided that he should stop paying Joni's sales royalties. He decided that it was the only way he could recoup the money invested in promoting her product. Joni of course had lived with Geffen for a couple of years (in the 1970s) so this also a termination of friendship and trust. I am not sure if Joni went to litigation once again to solve the problem but it is reported that David Geffen did finally repay those royalties to Joni; but did he regain her trust?

TURBULENT INDIGO (released November 1994)

The cover is an art exhibition in itself. One side of the compact disc sleeve unfolds to exhibit six framed paintings. The front cover is Joni's Van Gogh influenced portrait of herself, she has cut off her right ear, and bandaged it. As

Joni agreed when talking to Tracey McLeod on the B.B.C. Late Show, 'cobalt' was the colour of Van Gogh's skies and backgrounds, so why call the album 'indigo'. Joni made one of her most esoteric responses when she said.... "In a way that's where the term comes from - also its psychology, to be a great artist you have to be able to tap into emotional disturbances, channel them, you have to lasso the hurricane". Joni for some reason had also visited a psychic who had informed her that she was in her first incarnation as a woman. Previously she had been an English gentleman, then, a bird and an arab rug salesman, she seemed to consider these revelations with as much amusement as they deserved.

On the cover there is an art gallery of paintings. One of a canyon with a river running through it, a mountain range with a waterfall, two extremely blue seascapes, or lakescapes if there are such things. The one with the two small rocky islands may well be the rocks on which Joni was standing nude on the inner gatefold of the 'For the Roses' cover, they seem to be identical. Last but by far from least is a painting of a picnic table with two seats with straw squabs. It all combines to form a French impressionist painting, the apple tree, the table set for a party in the fields in summer. It is the only painting on show here where the signature can be observed, one can imagine this painting fetching a large sum in an auction, it really is excellent. The obverse of the fold-out has the lyrics and credits and three more paintings, two of mountains and sea, the other is probably Larry Klein, he has a cat on his right shoulder with its tail coiled around in front of his face, the cat's right paw is touching Larry's forehead. It is necessary to take the magnifying glass to this picture to see it properly. Finally there is a photograph of Joni smiling as she hold up the Joni (Van Gogh) painting, she is in her studio perched on the edge of the table that can be observed on the 'Wild Things Run Fast' cover, if not then it is very similar. She certainly doesn't look 51 years old. She has written a song called 'Happiness is The Best Facelift' (for release on a later album) from a remark made to her new man-friend, but Joni has been so often in the depths of love sick depression where are the frown lines? Here we have an album with such seriousness, there is no let up from the down-side.

SUNNY SUNDAY: An unhappy woman living in the endless hell of boredom, everyday is the same. She relieves her loneliness by shooting at the street light with her gun. Fictional Blanche Dubois is name checked, she was a sensitive southern American woman, she is haunted by the tragic marriage that warped her life. On a visit to her sister Stella's house she finds herself at loggerheads with Stanley Kowalsky, Stella's husband. Whilst Stella is in hospital having a baby Stanley rapes Blanche, her mind fails and she is taken to a mental hospital. I can only assume that Joni associated herself with Blanche Dubois over their failed marriages and the passing years. Blanche Dubois appears in Tennessee Williams' book 'A Streetcar Named Desire' published in 1947. Wayne Shorter is still in the band on saxophone and Jim Keltner adds some superb drumming.

SEX KILLS: Three verses which act as an update on Joni Mitchell's report on the state of the Los Angeles society. A car registration plate that says JUST ICE is the spark that ignited the lyric. The advertising agencies sell everything using sex, and it kills, according to Joni. The backing for the track is heavy and over-powering as is the loathing in the lyric. The Doctors give you the illness, then sell the cure-all pills, lawyers, rapists, cancer and the continuing plight of the Red Indians all pass through the lyric. Joni sounds as though she is becoming old and vindictive, surely life is not that bad?

HOW DO YOU STOP: Written by Charlie Midnight and Dan Hartman, it is a strange choice for Joni. It sounds like The Cars 'Drive' the song used as the theme song for the famine in Africa which was aided by Live Aid. Soul-disco singer Seal appears on backing vocal on a song for stopping before the excesses strike. It could be suicide, love, drugs anything, it may even be the problems of a genius or perhaps a person that thinks they are a genius.

TURBULENT INDIGO: A song for Vincent Van Gogh, or Van Go as the Americans prefer to call him, it is also easier to rhyme. Joni has painted her Van Gogh for the cover, complete with ear-bandage. Joni is presenting Gogh's mental anguish, his turbulent brain. His life has been frequently romanticised yet his paintings show little of the strain he was supposed to be suffering.

LAST CHANCE LOST: A simple but effective song sung with great conviction. It becomes like self-flagellation, two lovers dwelling on the pain at the end of their relationship. This is Larry's swan-song (swans sing just before they die), he started working with Joni on 'Wild Things Run Fast' in 1982, his time runs out here. Joni has rarely sung better than this, one of her most accomplished vocal outings, and a great song too.

THE MAGDALENE LAUNDRIES: Back on the theme of the unwanted pregnancy of the unmarried mother and the discarded child, this particular woman was 27. In the catholic church it is a major sin, here Joni waggles her index finger at the hypocrisy of it all. Pregnancy caused by the girl's father, or the priest. The church is supposed to give love and affection and according to Joni it breeds heartless hate. Mary Magdalene was assumed to be an unmarried mother, Jesus was born to a mother (another Mary not Mary Magdalene) who said that the child was conceived without sex, how could she be so sure, Joseph was not a celibate, or was he? Pregnant young girls locked away in the seminary and treated like prostitutes, destitutes, temptresses, all in the name of love and charity. Surely this is just a song, Joni can't believe these lyrics, there are no metaphors here, the lyric presents the case that nuns are conspiratorial in their denigration. This track is exalted in its potency, but is likely to change very little, as Joni says 'like a lame bulb that never blooms'. I am lost in admiration for the power of her use of so few words, Joni just improves with age. At Joni's appearance in The Great Musical Experience in Osaka, Japan, The Chieftains objected to this song so vociferously that they considered cancelling their show.

NOT TO BLAME: Is this for O.J. Simpson? The increasing male violence to women, yet this is only due to women at last having the courage to stand up and be heard, before they just suffered in silence. There is also child abuse and rape, two more crimes that have become more prevalent due to publicity and litigation. Once more Joni presents some horrific scenes in what sounds to be a gentle song. The male is never to blame, it might be pregnancy, assaults on children, the woman was always out-of-line, you, the men, were not to blame. As the last track on this album concerns The Book of Job from the Bible it is likely that Joni got her idea for this song from there; in Job 1:1 it states 'Man proved to be blameless'. The prevalent situation of male beating female and getting-away-with-it made the sentiments more powerful. We must remember that 12 jurors who heard all the evidence of O.J. Simpson decided that their was more than a shadow-of-doubt, and subsequently found him not guilty, only Simpson really knows the truth. If all the rest of the World thinks that O.J. was guilty then this leaves all women in an extremely precarious and hazardous predicament.

BORDERLINE: The line that is drawn which should not be breached, the chalk mark which can't be washed away. A song for the personal boundary that is drawn by each individual, or animal. On this track Joni has augmented the sound with Greg Leisz on pedal steel guitar, he hardly intrudes at all, it could have so easily been added by mixing in a keyboard effect.

YVETTE IN ENGLISH: It heralds the return of David Crosby as co-composer. In France, a free man in Paris, everything is possible in this metropolis. The offer of oral sex or marijuana from Yvette, signified in the sensual cigarette smoking, she is offering him instant bliss. This is a meeting that never reaches a substantial conclusion, she just walks off leaving him by The Seine. It could alternatively be a scene from a television advertisement.

THE SIRE OF SORROW (Job's Sad Song): After listening to 'Magdalene Laundries' where everything comes out whiter than white, it seems strange that Joni should now be advocating that we should never lose our faith. The trials of Job and his patience are compared with those of love and loss. The gulf between the two is so immense that they don't tolerate equal scrutiny. The antagonists point of view is shown in parenthesis in the lyric sheet as is Job's subtitle. Joni has created a conversation piece where she is answering the questions put by the inquisitor of Job.

One thing is certain, Joni has read the book of Job, however the quotes have all undergone considerable poetic adjustment. Firstly 'Sire of Sorrow' does not appear in Job. Job you may remember was the personification of poverty and patience. A 'Job's comforter'(and there are many about) is a person who when sympathizing with your grief says that you brought it on yourself, thus adding to your sorrow. In this book Job receives a great many rebukes from his so called comforters. I located some of Joni's excerpts from Job...

Job 7:11 'with the bitterness in my soul'.
Job 4:3 'Look! You have corrected many'.
Job 20:12 'bad tastes sweet in his mouth to melt away his tongue.
Job 31:6 'weigh me in accurate scales'.
Job 10:10 'and like cheeses to curdle me'.
Job 15:20 'a wicked one is suffering torture'.

All these appear somewhere in the song, but mostly in a different order, some of the adjustments completely change the meaning.

To promote the album Joni appeared on the B.B.C. Late Show in December, she sang 'Sunny Sunday' and 'Sex Kills'. She dressed in her trade mark beret which was now covering some grey hair, said show Producer Mark Cooper. At least she had not dyed it Mark, if you could see it then she didn't care. Mark Cooper also stated that she seemed to be 'without any apparent ego', well not many people have said that of Joni over the years, in fact I have not read any. Tracey McLeod conducted the interview with Joni which is more interesting than her 'Come in from the Cold' video. Joni details how the life in America has changed since the 1960s, it is far more aggressive nowadays. The hatred and jealousies are everywhere. Joni also sets the matter straight on her position on feminism. She likes men, all the feminists she has ever met hate men, it was always an us-and-them situation. Joni has spent most of her touring time with men, all her musicians are men, she was used to it and prefers it. I would have asked if she preferred to be the only woman with these men, (there is no competition), even when she employed a singing group to back her it was the all male Persuasions. Joni also accepted that female jazz singers were her role model, she mentions Lena Horne; remember Joni looked like Lena Horne on the cover of 'Don Juan's Reckless Daughter'.

A strong condemnation of the album came surprisingly from a female reviewer, Charlotte Greig for The Mojo Magazine. She thought the album had 'meandering songs', thought Joni was a 'doom laden seer', and her lyrics 'overwrought and ambiguous'. The article was titled 'The Charismatic Siren Gives Way to The Doom-laden Seer', so we knew what to expect. She presented some strange views indeed, she also thought 'Not to Blame' to be a 'dull anti-rape number'. My initial thoughts were that she just might be hard of hearing, or perhaps just not paying attention, ask any men just what they thought of that song. A song that concerns violence from a male against a female with O.J.Simpson's persona hovering over it like Banquo's ghost, has the least dull lyrics imaginable.

'Turbulent Indigo' sold well in U.K. reaching No 25, but there was another surprise in store for the album and Joni. The album won two Grammy Awards, one in the Best Pop Album category, the other for the cover design. I am sure that the art award pleased Joni more that she can say, rewarded for her painting achievements at last.

GHOSTS (1996)
HITS/MISSES (1996)

To put it vulgarly, the whole trouble with a folk song is that once you have played it through there is nothing much you can do except play it over again and play it rather louder.

Constant Lambert (1905-1951)

Joni played a live concert in New York on December 6th 1995. She was back in Greenwich Village after so many years. Joni was playing on a stratocaster electric guitar at the Fez Club. The audience was packed with stars old and new, Carly Simon, Eric Andersen and Chrissie Hynde were noticed by the Press.

Mother Myrtle was now acting as matchmaker. She introduced Joni to Donald Freed (born 1941) a librarian from Prince Albert, Saskatchewan, Canada, he is two years older than Joni. Prince Albert was as close to Saskatoon as North Battleford where Joni was for a time in her youth, Prince Albert is more northern, the last reasonable sized town before Canadian nothingness. The tributaries of The Saskatchewan River connect Prince Albert, Saskatoon and North Battleford, it was like Joni and Donald were destined to meet each other. Donald Freed was also writing songs and started collaborating with Joni.

Probably the most exciting thing that Joni could have wanted actually happened. She was finally reunited with her daughter Kelly although she is now named Kilauren, she is married. Joni had an extra surprise to find that she is also a grandmother, she has a grandson. They say 'like mother like daughter', well Kilauren like Joni has been a rebellious child, she left home at 14 to see the world with her brother.

HITS/MISSES (released late 1996)

Released as two separate albums, both of the covers have photos by Norman Seef taken from the same session. Joni is chalk marking the ground, drawing a car and a body shape, like the police draw around the body at a murder scene. Joni lays down within the body drawing. The cover of HITS shows her lying down , MISSES drawing the car. The 'Hits' set includes on album for the first time by JONI 'Urge For Going' which is an acoustic solo studio version apparently recorded at the time of the first album but only used as a B-Side. We were awaiting a boxed set of Joni's best sides coupled with out-takes and rarities, this seems to have been shelved in favour of two albums with just 'Urge for Going' as the reason for fans to purchase 'Hits'.

In 1996 Alison Anders who was directing the film 'Grace of My Heart' asked Joni to write and record a song for the soundtrack. The film was based loosely on the life and times of singer composer Carole King. Joni wrote 'Man From Mars', it was initially agreed that Joni would appear in the film, and certainly she would be included on the soundtrack album. The leading actress in the film was Ileana Douglas and her singing voice on other songs in the film were over-dubbed by Kristen Vigard. To maintain continuity Joni's version was not used and Kristen Vigard was asked to sing the song. The original soundtrack was released including Joni's version of the song, which of course did not now appear in the film. The shops were already selling the album and as many as 2000 were thought to have been pressed which included Joni's version. It is the second edition of the soundtrack that has Kristen Vigard's version, Joni's has been removed. The 'Grace of My Heart' soundtrack was composed by Burt Bacharach and Elvis Costello and released as 'God Give Me Strength'. This title could not be the pleas of either composer as they followed-up the album two years later with another collaboration titled 'Painted From Memory'.

GHOSTS (Essential-Outlaw released 1996)

Almost by chance I stumbled across GHOSTS which is a live album on Outlaw Records. It is advertised in the music shop Bible 'Laserlog' as freely available but has all the signs of being illicit, which it probably isn't, they wouldn't sell it, would they? It was released in 1996 and has a double exposure photograph on the cover. This is a side view of Joni with straight long hair which gives the impression that she is a Red Indian; she looks similar to singer Essra Mohawk on her first album cover. (Essra Mohawk is also Sandy Hurvitz who made an album with Frank Zappa at the time of his involvement with The G.T.Os). The picture on 'Ghosts' is set over clouds and a hazy light-blue sky. The inner of the sleeve has a photograph from The Last Waltz Show showing Joni with Neil Young and Robbie Robertson (it may be Bob Dylan), and a separate smiling photo of Joni. The blurb states...'In tribute to that ground breaking album Outlaw Records bring you GHOSTS, featuring rare versions of songs from 'The Ladies of the Canyon' album, never heard before. This collection contains (10) live performances, television and radio broadcasts taken from 1969 to 1971'.

On listening to the album it becomes obvious that this is not all it seems. The tracks are all slightly shorter than the original studio album, it may just be that they were recorded from a record player which was spinning at 35 rpm, the recording sound is also more 'airy'. What makes matters worse is that it is 'The Ladies of the Canyon' album, even Joni's laugh at the end of 'Big Yellow Taxi' is absolutely identical, she couldn't have managed that exactly the same twice. Sold at under £7.00 one wonders just what the liner notes are meant to convey to any Joni Mitchell collector that hopes that they have found something new and different. I know that bootleg records are often available of live shows recorded badly and sold illegally, but this is the first time that I have come across an album that is the original re-recorded badly and just put out on compact disc with the tracks in a different order to confuse the purchaser. I did some investigations, (because this was available at any record shop), the distributor has subsequently suspended sales, frozen their stock, and they informed me that Outlaw Records was in now receivership. As an added mystery why pick this album for this illicit release surely there are far more lucrative choices, it is like a postage stamp counterfeiter choosing the 5p stamp to produce rather than copy the £5.00.

The management relationship between Peter Asher and Joni ended after 14 years, so as she had 17 years with Elliot Roberts 31 years with just two men must be considered responsible by anyone's standards. Joni has also received more awards such as The Billboard Century Award, The National Academy of Songwriter's Achievement Award, The Canadian Governor General's Performing Arts Award (Joni admitted to Dave DiMartino that she blushed like a schoolgirl when she received it), and The Swedish Polar Music Prize. She has also been elected to The Rock 'n' Roll Hall of Fame. The award was presented to her by Graham Nash on stage during her 1998 shows with Bob Dylan and Van Morrison. One of the members of the band had been looking at the award the day before and accidentally dropped it, the top part had broken off. Graham presented the award to Joni in a 'rubbish bag', this amused Joni who still considers that the industry froze her out for years. Joni felt that she could not go to the ceremony and be humble with copious 'thank-you's' so apparently the 'Hall of Fame' delayed the honour for three years hoping that she would change her mind, they should have realised that flexibility is not one of Joni's attributes, the 'Hall of Fame' relented anyway. The commerciality of The Hall of Fame events was also one of the reasons that Joni refused to attend, in an interview in Mojo magazine she said that to take her family to witness the achievement would have cost her $20,000, if this is true that is why they give the award to different people each year!

As mentioned earlier Joni appeared on a seven date concert tour with Bob Dylan and Van Morrison, and also appeared in an all woman show at The Wiltern Theatre on April 16th 1998. Joni was not feeling well for a couple of the shows but in the best trouper tradition appeared anyway and gave her best, hardly anyone would have realised she was not well. Van Morrison opened the show wearing his 'structured' jacket and black hat. The jacket is a tailored creation that is designed to cover his corpulence and not show creases in the powerful lights. In deference to the recently departed Frank Sinatra, Van sang 'That's Life' a song that sounds more comfortable in his vocal chords than Frank's. He also sang Sly Stone's 'Thank You Falettinme Be Mice Elf Again'. Bob Dylan who closed the show sang 'Restless Farewell' for Frank, Bob had sung (or perhaps mumbled is a better description) the same song three years earlier at Sinatra's 80th birthday tribute show.

Joni sang songs from her post 'Hejira' period, songs with less melody but more rhythm. Joni sang her Bob Dylan impersonation on 'his' verse of 'Big Yellow Taxi', she has never mastered the Dylan voice as well as Joan Baez did on her version of 'Simple Twist of Fate'. In Joni's version of 'Hejira' she added a line about Frank Sinatra, so on the evening concerned they had the ghost of Frank in their hearts. Joni premiered a couple of songs from her forthcoming album, these were 'Facelift' and 'The Crazy Cries of Love'. An evening where the three of the greatest singer songwriters in the history of popular music were on the stage in the same show, it only needed Leonard Cohen to forsake his Buddhist robes for a day to make it the strongest ever show, in my humble opinion of course.

In an all-woman-show Joni appeared with Bjork, Stevie Nicks, Sheryl Crow, Trisha Yearwood and others for The Los Angeles Walden Woods Benefit. In the photographs of her on stage with Bjork, Joni is wearing a stylish dark grey dress with padded shoulders, she looks more beautiful than ever. Joni achieved another of her ambitions at this show when she sang 'Stormy Weather' with an exhilarating 60 piece orchestra. She enjoyed the experience so much she agreed to sing some Gershwin songs on jazz pianist Herbie Hancock's album, as yet un-released.

TAMING THE TIGER (1998)

Music produces the kind of pleasure which
human nature can not do without.
                                    Confucius (551-479BC)

Joni, like so many others, has been diagnosed as suffering from 'Post Polio Syndrome'. For many years she controlled the seizing-up of joints with swimming and Yoga exercises, but natural ageing and stress adds to the problems with muscle and joint spasms. Apparently the syndrome attacks many sufferers (Joni included) in another manner, the body temperature control is erratic causing the body system an inability to accurately regulate body heat. This is of course aggravated by pressurised air-travel. Swimming still remains Joni's favourite therapy, she can just float and exercise her joints, and of course her smoke coated lungs.

Janet Jackson decided to sample Joni's 'Big Yellow Taxi' and add her own dance backing to the song. It was released as a single and became a hit, it also appeared on Janet's 1997 'The Velvet Rope' album. The track sampling is credited on the sleeve with the track stating that it features Joni Mitchell and Q-Tip.

The layman's idea that Joni appeared at the original Woodstock Festival remains in the psyche. Woodstock will celebrate its 30th anniversary in 1999 but an alternative Woodstock was celebrated in 1998. The festival called 'A Day in the Garden' was deemed a resounding success. Mojo Magazine reported that veterans from 1969 attended this show namely Peter Townshend, Ten Years After, Melanie, Richie Havens and Joni Mitchell. There was a picture of Pete, Joni and Richie smiling, but the festival was not all smiles. A thousand protestors grouped under the name of 'Friends of The Farm' petitioned the 70,000 crowd against Alan Gerry, the cable television billionaire who owns the land. The reason for the protest was that Alan Gerry one of the richest men in America wants to develop the site into a cultural music and performing arts complex. The protestors believe that Gerry's commercial instinct will run against the spirit of the original event. Surely these purists realise that this is progress, they had 30 years in which they could have bought the land, I expect they too would have seen the commercial potential by now of a fallow field. Pete Townshend mooted that there would be a 30th anniversary festival.

TAMING THE TIGER (released September 1998)

The title track of 'Wild Things Run Fast' was Joni's own interpretation of The taming of the Shrew in reverse, in that song she thought that she had her man tamed. The album cover is a painting of Joni holding up a cat. Joni wearing a straw hat is standing in a garden, the signature shows that it was painted in 1997. Brian Hinton describes Joni's (and Van Morrison's) voice as sounding like a 'feral cat', which may not be complimentary, but here on the cover we have Joni with cat, her bonsai tiger, yet her voice is more mature and mellow than ever. The sleeve design for 'Turbulent Indigo' won an award for design, the 'Taming the Tiger' booklet is even better. The paintings are extraordinary. On page three we have a figure (probably Joni) sitting on a river bank at sunset, a windmill can be seen in the distance. She has a play-on-words around the frame which states Idol-Idle-Idyll-Ideal. A landscape on page 5, a cat on page 7 which could have been part of a painting by Henri Rousseau. Page 9 has a portrait of Donald Freed reading, the lighting of the painting is superb. There is a painting of a lady (Joni) on a park bench with a man's hand holding her leg which is particularly clever, painted from the man's eye-view. In another Joni sits at the side of a river wearing the straw hat shown on the cover, looking towards a major city. The eye is led into the picture by the half side face and shoulder of a man. The art gallery continues with Joni face-to-face with a deer, this is followed by a seascape. The rear of the booklet has a cat laying on a patterned sheet set against three flower vases. The rear of the jewel box is a photograph of a cat standing on a table. There is another superb snow-scene landscape hanging on the wall; any artist will tell you how difficult it is to paint snow-scenes. The multitude of riches is increased as the compact disc itself shows the cat sitting-up on a bed with the table from the rear photograph in the rear. Removing the CD exposes the same picture in the back of the jewel box. Joni has absorbed the styles of Rousseau, Cezanne, Manet, Gauguin and others but her paintings never appear to be impressionistic. There can rarely have been a more beautiful presentation, and this is all before we hear the music

Joni's selection of a cat/tiger for the album sets her in excellent company with artists, singers, poets and actresses that have previously used cats. Goya, Picasso and of course the eccentric Louis Wain were cat painters, Wain even lived like a cat, he only drank from a saucer. W.B. Yeats wrote 'Cat on the Moon'. Eartha Kitt made her name acting the cat, she also played catwoman in the Adam West TV Batman series. Emma Peel (Diana Rigg) wore a cat suit and Mrs Peel (Honor Blackman) went from leather clothes to playing Pussey Galore with Sean Connery's James Bond. Of course cats have a connection with Jazz, as in 'cool cats' and the affectionate name for the girlfriends of jazzmen has always been 'Jazz Kitty'.

From the booklet notes it is evident that Joni's desire to make music again was rekindled by Fred Wallecki and Brian Blade, Blade plays drums on the album. Joni has now moved from guitar to synthesizer, although on some tracks she plays both and bass. The overall sound of the album is pristine and perfect, but the synthesised sounds have taken over. Wayne Shorter remains on saxophone, Greg Leisz adds pedal steel guitar although at times he is mixed so far back he is hard to hear, Larry Klein adds bass to three tracks. Joni also has new managers who are credited on the sleeve, Steve Macklam and Sam Feldman. So after 4 years break we get 40 minutes of songs, ten minutes per year.

HARLEM IN HAVANA: It is introduced by synthesized metallic sounds which are sequenced with crowd noises and a 'guitar orchestra', probably over-layered by Joni on the synthesizer. Wayne Shorter's saxophone fights its way through the clamour as Joni sings the song of a girl that got a part in a black revue after leaving home. We have a burlesque barker in Femi Jiya calling "Step right up folks!" The girl Emmy May and her trumpet playing black man are appearing at The Havana Club, Harlem, or this may be reversed to be The Harlem Club, Havana. Emmy has dyed her hair blonde, she has the dangling spangles, she is under age. The song is for two girls because Joni writes that 'we were under age', so Joni may be the other girl that does not do a strip-tease. The rejoinder is that Auntie Ruthie would not have approved, that is if she had known. This was the scenario presented for the song some months ago but on investigation it appears to be far more innocent. Two girls who managed to get into the burlesque show at the circus when they are under-aged. The excitement for the girls is that they have done this without the knowledge of their Aunt Ruthie. Larry Klein's fretless bass continues to sound like Jaco Pastorius on a superb opening song.

MAN FROM MARS: This is the song written for the film 'Grace of My Heart'. A slow love song, Joni plays all the instruments except for Brian Blade on drums. The man from Mars might just be out of reach, he went too far and broke her heart, she cries every day. She is alone again, I love the line that he was 'swallowed by the dark' as he left her. A superb slow love song. It was suggested amusingly to me that perhaps she was a chocaholic waiting for the salesman from Mars to arrive!

LOVE PUTS ON A NEW FACE: Love has many faces, sides, one letter would change this to facets. Joni sets the chorus of this song in France, once again. The backing track is excellent as is the lyric, it deserved a better tune. The meeting, the silence as love grows. She is unhappy and he worries over the reason. She is feeling torn apart, Joni uses alligator jaws and beast of prey as her metaphors. The meeting (or perhaps another meeting) in France where every day is different, I am unsure of the relevance of France to the lyric, but Joni loves to set her scenes there. In the first verse the seduction scene is set, but seems that it was not consummated. The second verse has the questioning, and the third is his letter of longing for her. Probably love does put on a new face but re-activates an old one, or another of its facets.

LEAD BALLOON: Is as near as Joni gets to rock 'n' roll. We don't get any clues of whom this song refers. Joni certainly has an 'Irish' temper, she throws her tequila over a businessman, surely not poor old David Geffen again. 'Kiss my Ass' she says to him, and he owns the town. He has the heart of a frozen fish. What we learn is that an angry woman is a match for an angry man, if that woman is Joni. There are similarities here to the feminine aggression displayed by the songs of Alanis Morissette, Joni may have listened to her work. The band on this track sound like Weather Report, and they get room to flex their jazz tendencies. This lyric may be Joni still angry on the way she was frozen out by the music business. He say's "Sic her Rover", which is the American term for inciting a dog to attack. In the U.K. we would say 'Seize her Rover'. It is curious to add that the other term for 'sic' a reference that 'an odd or questionable reading of an point or item is fact'. So was Joni frozen out or not she was always stating that she was retiring from music, perhaps the industry thought she had...(sic).

NO APOLOGIES: It was reported that this track was inspired by Joni reading of a Japanese girl raped by U.S. troops in Yokohama. That fact is confirmed by the first verse, but then Joni moves on to her thoughts on lawyers and loan sharks, drug lords and warlords. Juan returns although there seems to be no connection with Don Juan's reckless daughter. The O.J.Simpson acquittal obviously upset Joni considerably. Here again Joni is under the impression that women get a bad deal because it is the men that decide. Joni also uses 'snakes and snails and puppy dogs tails' in the lyric and I commented on that in the earlier title track of 'Don Juan's Reckless Daughter'.. This is Joni's hopelessness with the poor ecological situation due to governments and their monetary desires.

TAMING THE TIGER: Joni back in stream of consciousness mode. The coyotes and wolves from the previous albums have been replaced by felines. William Blake's 'tiger tiger burning bright' is the springboard for the lyric. Joni is the tiger, perhaps she feels that at last she is tamed just like Shakespeare's shrew. She does not compromise on 'the whining white kids of the record biz', although Joni considers that she is now a runaway from the 'record-biz'. She is looking at the stars and musing her position, and the conclusion is that it has all got boring. Of course 'tiger' may be a metaphor for 'desire' or even 'the urge'. If 'Urge' is substituted for tiger in the lyric then it may refer to the taming of libido or the wanderlust, her 'urge for going'.

THE CRAZY CRIES OF LOVE: Lyrics written by Donald Freed, and good they are too. The saxophone sounds like a train whistle mentioned in the lyric. The lyric is for the ecstasy of love and the realisation that no-one can hear. The lover's time their climaxes with the sound of the passing train so an eavesdropper will not hear. This is an optimistic song of love, they are totally engrossed in each other, but why are they paranoid that the folks above won't hear; perhaps they are staying at Myrtle's house, so much for 'taming the urge'.

STAY IN TOUCH: The lyrics are set across the page in the lyric booklet to the park bench painting, the man is holding the lady's leg. Unlikely to be by chance for this gives the lyrics two viewpoints. Two lovers parting or alternatively a call to Joni's daughter Kilauren to 'Stay in Touch'. The album is dedicated to daughter Kilauren and grandson Marlin for 'just being in this world'. A plea from the heart sung beautifully. Joni has painted the arm of a man showing him wearing a dark jacket which suggests that the song is a message to a lover.

FACE LIFT: Here Joni implores her mother to leave her and new man Donald alone. Myrtle had introduced them to each other, yet she continues to be prudish about Joni's relationships. Surely she can't feel the disgrace with modern day morals, Myrtle is now a great-grandmother, thanks to Joni. The song was premiered four years ago, the title taken from a chance remark. Joni realises that she is now middle aged but is living with a man whilst not been married. This has happened to Joni for many years, she only married Larry Klein, so why does Myrtle continue to pour scorn on her relationships? Joni refers to it as Myrtle's 'Sacred Cow'. I think that maybe it is Joni who by her mothers's inferences, feels the disgrace, it makes the previous track more pertinent. Joni has absorbed so many unfair remarks concerning her relationships that many have been integrated within her psyche, and here she pours them out, with Myrtle as the person for whom she has felt the pain as she has searched for own happiness. It is true that Myrtle is a powerful personality in herself, Joni has inherited her genes, if they are too alike then friction will occur, but surely Joni is just using the situation the exorcise ghosts again. But why does Myrtle say that Joni had come home to disgrace 'us'. At least Joni argues back with the remark, (or the question), 'Why is joy not allowed'. Again the listener feels that they are intruding in a family rift of which we are illicit eavesdroppers.

MY BEST TO YOU: Sung as a very slow waltz, almost hymnal. The catchiest song on the album, every day is a gift from heaven, make your dreams come true, the smiles and the tears are all part of life's rich pattern. This was written by Isham Jones and Gene Willadsen in 1942, and Joni's interpretation of the lyric makes it sound like a belated blessing from a grandmother. Isham Jones and his orchestra were very popular in 1924, in fact he had a popular hit with 'My Best Girl', Jones composed (amongst others), 'It Had to be You', 'Broken Hearted Melody' and 'The One I Love Belongs to Somebody Else'; I could not find 'My Best to You' listed. The 'Sons of the Pioneers' recorded a song of the same name years ago, I can not confirm or deny if it was the same song.

TIGER BONES: This is just studio filler, after four years Joni only has enough songs to last 40 minutes. This is a four minute backing track which needs a vocal. My CD also has a long gap between this and the penultimate track, stretching out the overall time of the disc.

David Hepworth reviewing for Mojo Magazine probably doesn't like the album, he remarks on the tracks but doesn't say anything positive. Neil McCormack reviewing for the Daily Telegraph wrote 'Female singer songwriters have never been in greater demand, so it is nice to welcome back the original, and indeed, the greatest of them all to show everyone how it should be done'. McCormack concurs with my Alanis Morissette views on the track 'Lead balloon'. He continues by inferring that Joni's jazzy rhythms and sophisticated lyrics are too complex for mass consumption, he also thinks that Joni has never achieved 'rock goddess' status, because she doesn't play 'rock'; 'Pop Goddess' doesn't have the same panache, does it.

We still await the accolade of a Joni Mitchell boxed set. It was mooted a few years ago but we got 'Hits' and 'Misses' instead which was not what the fans were waiting for, a set of out-takes, re-mixes and discarded songs set out in a box similar to the magnificent C.S.N. set would be ideal, we live in hope.

David Crosby once said of Joni that she is as 'modest as Mussolini'. She realises that her confidence has often been misconstrued as arrogance, but a woman surviving in an industry run by males she needs to be tougher than all the men. She can give the appearance of a wilting flower but retain her inner strength, she needs it to endure, add to that perseverance and one has Joni Mitchell in a nutshell. She has had many relationships but she has always chosen her men well. As far as I can ascertain none of her former lovers has gone into print dishing-the-dirt, they have all remained friends, which is no mean achievement in any situation, let alone the music industry.

Although she did have a child once, her replies to the question of consummating marriages with children have often received evasive responses. In her media search for Kelly (Kilauren) she said "I just want to tell her, I didn't give her up for the lack of love". Another reply to the question of her having her own children was that she had lots of Godchildren, and the children of friends: reading between the lines that meant that she wished that she had more of her own. One thing that would have proved more difficult was her friendly relationships with her past lovers would have been harder to maintain on friendly terms if children had to be argued over and shared.

This may be Joni's last album, it seems that she took a great deal of persuading to make 'Taming of the Tiger'. Whatever Joni decides to do in the future her position as one of the greatest will remain, not only in the hierarchy of pop music but in all our hearts. I suppose I need a syrupy embarrassing ending to this book so I must explain that the title for this book was selected for two reasons. One it is the two words mostly associated with Joni, but more importantly the fact that Joni has always searched for her own private paradise. Just like Dorothy venturing up the yellow brick road (also paved) in search of happiness, only to find it in her own back yard. Joni's friendships turned to love and then back to friendships, there seems to be very little (if any) malice on either side of those relationships. She has found stability with Donald Freed, we can only hope on her behalf that she has at last found her own paradise paved in happiness.

Good luck Joni Mitchell, at least now she knows where she stands!

TRACK FINDER

All I Want/Blue-Miles of Aisles
Amelia/Hejira-Shadows and Light
Arrangement/Ladies of the Canyon-Misses

Baby I Don't Care/Wild Things Run Fast
Banquet/For the Roses
Barangrill/For the Roses
Beat of Black Wings/Chalk Mark-Misses
Be Cool/Wild Things Run Fast
Big Yellow Taxi/Ladies of the Canyon-Miles of Aisles-Hits
Bird that Whistles (Corrina Corrina)/Chalk Mark
Black Crow/Hejira-Shadows and Light
Blonde in the Bleachers/For the Roses
Blue/Blue-Miles of Aisles
Blue Boy/Ladies of the Canyon
Blue Motel Room/Hejira
Boho Dance/Hissing of Summer
Borderline/Turbulent Indigo
Both Sides Now/Clouds-Miles of Aisles-Hits

Cactus Tree/Song to a Seagull-Miles of Aisles
California/Blue-Hits
Carey/Blue-Miles of Aisles-Hits
Car on the Hill/Court and Spark
Case of You/Blue-Miles of Aisles-Misses
Centrepiece/Hissing of Summer
Chair in the Sky/Mingus
Chelsea Morning/Clouds-Hits
Cherokee Louise/Night Ride Home
Chinese Cafe/Wild Things Run Fast-Hits
Circle Game/Ladies of the Canyon-Miles of Aisles-Hits
Coin in the Pocket (Rap)/Mingus
Cold Blue Steel and Sweet Fire/For the Roses-Miles of Aisles
Cool Water/Chalk Mark
Come in From the Cold/Night Ride Home-Hits
Conversation/Ladies of the Canyon
Cotton Avenue/Don Juan's
Court and Spark/Court and Spark
Coyote/Hejira-Shadows and Light
Crazy Cries of Love/Taming the Tiger

Dancing Clown/Chalk Mark
Dawntreader/Song to a Seagull
Dog Eat Dog/Dog Eat Dog-Misses
Don Juan's Reckless Daughter/Don Juan's
Don't Interrupt the Sorrow/Hissing of Summer
Down to You/Court and Spark
Dreamland/Don Juan's-Shadows and Light
Dry Cleaner From Des Moines/Mingus-Shadows and Light

Edith and the Kingpin/Hissing of Summer-Shadows and Light
Electricity/For the Roses

Ethiopia/Dog Eat Dog

Face lift/Taming the Tiger
Fiction/Dog Eat Dog
Fiddle and the Drum/Clouds
For Free/Ladies of the Canyon
For the Roses/For the Roses-Misses
Free Man in Paris/Court and Spark-Shadows and Light-Hits
Funeral (Rap)/Mingus
Furry Sings the Blues/Hejira-Shadows and Light

Gallery/Clouds
God Must Be a Boogie Man/Mingus-Shadows and Light
Goodbye Pork Pie Hat/Mingus-Shadows and Light
Good Friends/Dog Eat Dog

Happy Birthday 1975 (RAP)/Mingus
Harlem in Havana/Taming the Tiger
Harry's House/Hissing of Summer-Misses
Hejira/Hejira-Shadows and Light-Misses
Help Me/Court and Spark-Hits
Hissing of Summer Lawns/Hissing of Summer
How Do You Stop/Turbulent Indigo

I Don't Know Where I Stand/Clouds
I Had a King/Song to a Seagull
In France They Kiss on Main Street/Hissing of Summer-Shadows and Light
Impossible Dreamer/Dog Eat Dog-Misses
I's a Muggin' (Rap)/Mingus
I Think I Understand/Clouds

Jericho/Miles of Aisles-Don Juan's
Judgement of the Moon and Stars (Ludwig's Tune)/For the Roses
Jungle Line/Hissing of Summer
Just Like This Train/Court and Spark

Ladies Man/Wild Things Run Fast
Ladies of the Canyon/Ladies of the Canyon
Lakota/Chalk Mark
Last Chance Lost/Turbulent Indigo
Last Time I Saw Richard/Blue-Miles of Aisles
Lay Down Your Arms/Chalk Mark
Lead Balloon/Taming the Tiger
Lesson in Survival/For the Roses
Let the Wind Carry Me/For the Roses
Little Green/Blue
Love/Wild Things Run Fast
Love or Money/Miles of Aisles
Love Puts on a New Face/Taming the Tiger
Lucky (Rap)/Mingus
Lucky Girl/Dog Eat Dog

Magdalene Laundries/Turbulent Indigo-Misses
Man From Mars/Taming the Tiger
Man to Man/Wild Things Run Fast

Marcie/Song to a Seagull
Michael of the Mountains/Song to a Seagull
Moon at the Window/Wild Things Run Fast
Morning Morgantown/Ladies of the Canyon
My Best to You/Taming the Tiger
My Old Man/Blue
My Secret Place/Chalk Mark

Nathan La Franeer/Song to a Seagull
Night in the City/Song to a Seagull
Night Ride Home/Night Ride Home
No Apologies/Taming the Tiger
Nothing Can Be Done/Night Ride Home-Misses
Not to Blame/Turbulent Indigo
Number One/Chalk Mark

Off Night Backstreet/Don Juan's
Only Joy in Town/Night Ride Home
Otis and Marlena/Don Juan's

Paprika Plains/Don Juan's
Passion Play(When All the Slaves are Free)/Night Ride Home-Misses
People's Parties/Court and Spark-Miles of Aisles
Pirate of Penance/Song to a Seagull

Priest/Ladies of the Canyon

Rainy Night House/Ladies of the Canyon-Miles of Aisles
Raised on Robbery/Court and Spark-Hits
Ray's Dad's Cadillac/Night Ride Home
Real Good For Free (For Free)/Miles of Aisles
Refuge of the Roads/Hejira
Reoccurring Dream/Chalk Mark-Misses
River/Blue-Hits
Roses Blue/Clouds

Same Situation/Court and Spark
See You Sometime/For the Roses
Sex Kills/Turbulent Indigo-Misses
Shades of Scarlett Conquering/Hissing of Summer
Shadows and Light/Hissing of Summer-Shadows and Light
Shiny Toys/Dog Eat Dog
Silky Veils of Ardor/Don Juan's
Sire of Sorrow (Job's Sad Song)/Turbulent Indigo
Sisotowbell Lane/Song to a Seagull
Slouching Towards Bethlehem/Night Ride Home
Smokin' (Empty Try Another)/Dog Eat Dog
Snakes and Ladders/Chalk Mark
Solid Love/Wild Things Run Fast
Song For Sharon/Hejira
Songs to Aging Children Come/Clouds
Song to a Seagull/Song to a Seagull
Stay in Touch/Taming the Tiger
Strange Boy/Hejira
Sunny Sunday/Turbulent Indigo

Sweet Bird/Hissing of Summer
Sweet Sucker Dance/Mingus

Talk to Me/Don Juan's
Taming the Tiger/Taming the Tiger
Tax Free/Dog Eat Dog
Tea Leaf Prophecy/Chalk Mark
Tenth World/Don Juan's
That Song About Midway/Clouds
This Flight Tonight/Blue
Three Great Stimulants/Dog Eat Dog
Tiger Bones/Taming the Tiger
Tin Angel/Clouds
Troubled Child/Court and Spark
Twisted/Court and Spark
Two Grey Rooms/Night Ride Home

Unchained Melody/Wild Things Run fast
Underneath the Streetlight/Wild Things Run Fast
Urge For Going/Hits

Why Do Fools Fall in Love/Shadows and Light
Wild Things Run Fast/Wild Things Run Fast
Willy/Ladies of the Canyon
Windfall (Everything for Nothing)/Night Ride Home
Wolf that Lives in Lindsey/Mingus-Misses
Woman of Heart and Mind/For the Roses-Miles of Aisles
Woodstock/Ladies of the Canyon-Miles of Aisles-Shadows and Light-Hits

You Dream Flat Tires/Wild Things Run Fast
You're So Square/Wild Things Run Fast
You Turn me On, I'm a Radio/For the Roses-Miles of Aisles-Hits
Yvette in English/Turbulent Indigo

ACKNOWLEDGEMENTS

BOOKS

Guinness Book of Rock Stars/
                    Dafyydd Rees and Luke Crampton, Guinness Books.
Joni Mitchell-Both sides Now by Brian Hinton, Sanctuary Books.

ARTICLES AND REVIEWS

Timothy White/Billboard Magazine
Nick Kent/NME
Ray Coleman/Evening Standard
Paul Barrera/Art Beat Reader Magazine
Stephen Holden/Rolling Stone Magazine
Rolling Stone Magazine
Barney Hoskyns/MOJO
Janet Maslin/Rolling Stone Magazine
Phil Sutcliffe/Q Magazine
Max Bell/NME
Lucy O'Brien/She Bop, Penguin Books
Richard Skinner/BBC 2
Jon Landau/Rolling Stone Magazine
Ariel Swartley/Rolling Stone Magazine
Mick Brown/Telegraph Colour Supplement
Dave Wilson/Broadside Magazine
Tim Lott/Sounds
Debbie Pead/Record Collector
Andy DiMartino/Mojo Magazine
Charlotte Greig/Mojo Magazine
Cameron Crowe/Rolling Stone Interviews 1979 + 1981

Not forgetting help beyond the call of duty from....

.....Rob Nicholls, Ken Brooks, Ben Cruikshank, Jack Rostill, Mike Edwards, Harry Allen, Jenny Keefe, David Housden, Tony Coleman, David Brooks and Margaret Lamont.

Cover design and watercolour collaged illustrations courtesy of
                                      Ken Brooks and Music (UK) Ltd

CURRENT TITLE

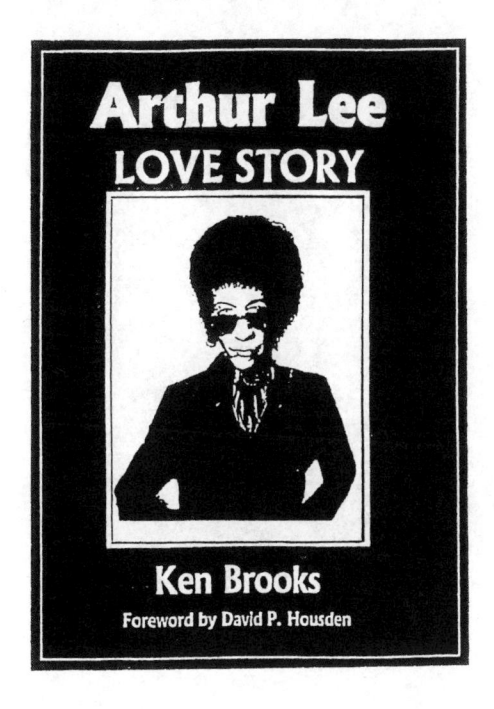

Arthur Lee
LOVE STORY

Ken Brooks
Foreword by David P. Housden

ARTHUR LEE LOVE STORY. A genius, an innovator, an enigma. Arthur Lee's group LOVE recorded one of the greatest albums in the history of popular music, 'Forever Changes'. He never allowed his music to stagnate, his changes in direction and music styles made him difficult to categorise. All his officially released albums are reviewed track-by-track, with the addition of some later semi-official live recordings. Arthur Lee is at present serving time in an American prison under the three strikes and out legislation. This book presents Arthur as a great musician whose work has sometimes exhilarating, sometime exasperating, but never less than interesting.

ARTHUR LEE, LOVE STORY
ISBN 1 899882 60 X
Paperback 210 x 150mm PRICE £5.99

AGENDA LIMITED, UNITS 1 & 2, LUDGERSHALL BUSINESS PARK, NEW DROVE, LUDGERSHALL, ANDOVER, HAMPSHIRE SP11 9RN

CURRENT TITLE

The pop sixties is nostalgia personified, the music of the sixties will last forever. It was a time when pop music germinated to engulf psychedelia creating a new adolescence awareness. Here in this book Kelvin Holmes has compiled a celebration of music which stretches across a wide spectrum, he has compiled his own 'Family Trees' and documented chart successes in both UK and USA. The book includes..The Animals, Byrds, Kinks, Beach Boys, Manfred Mann, Zombies, Steve Miller, Small faces, Searchers, Troggs, Move, Mojos, Hollies, Canned Heat, Creedence Clearwater, Dion, Procol Harum, Them, McCoys, and many more.

MY GENERATION
ISBN 1 899882 80 4
Paperback 210 x 150mm £ 7.99

AGENDA LIMITED, UNITS 1 & 2, LUDGERSHALL BUSINESS PARK,
NEW DROVE, LUDGERSHALL, ANDOVER, HAMPSHIRE, SP11 9RN

CURRENT TITLE

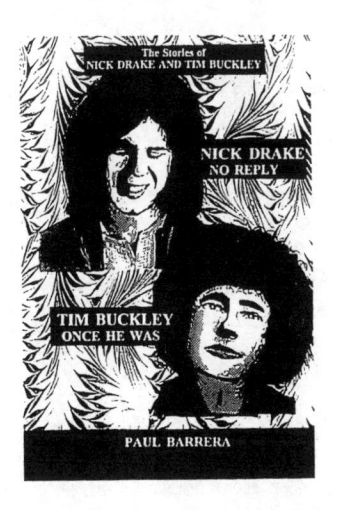

Tim Buckley and Nick Drake two prodigious and precocious talents who died far too young. Neither managed to achieve the success they so rightly deserved during their lifetime. Tim Buckley did change his musical direction in search of fame and fortune, but the critics who had criticised his earlier work turned against him claiming that he had 'sold-out' in search of financial success. Nick Drake only released three albums and never lived long enough to follow an alternative route to stardom, he was artistically incorruptible so it is unlikely that he would have modified his ideals towards a more accessible pop music.

Both Tim and Nick had an instinctive dramatic construction of lyrics, Tim's live performances were wild and emotional, Nick's quiet and reflective. They have both continued to reach new generations of listeners posthumously, they both died of drug excess one from Heroin the other from Tryptizol.

This book re-examines their careers and re-reviews every track on every album by the two singer song-writers.

NICK DRAKE/NO REPLY...TIM BUCKLEY/ONCE HE WAS,
a 2-in-1 book ISBN 1 899882 55 3.
Paperback 210 x 150mm PRICE £5.99

AGENDA LIMITED, UNITS 1 & 2, LUDGERSHALL BUSINESS PARK,
NEW DROVE, LUDGERSHALL, ANDOVER, HAMPSHIRE SP11 9RN

BOOKS FOR SALE

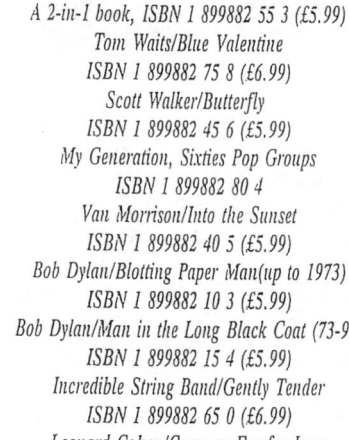

Nick Drake-No Reply/Tim Buckley-Once he Was
A 2-in-1 book, ISBN 1 899882 55 3 (£5.99)
Tom Waits/Blue Valentine
ISBN 1 899882 75 8 (£6.99)
Scott Walker/Butterfly
ISBN 1 899882 45 6 (£5.99)
My Generation, Sixties Pop Groups
ISBN 1 899882 80 4
Van Morrison/Into the Sunset
ISBN 1 899882 40 5 (£5.99)
Bob Dylan/Blotting Paper Man(up to 1973)
ISBN 1 899882 10 3 (£5.99)
Bob Dylan/Man in the Long Black Coat (73-93)
ISBN 1 899882 15 4 (£5.99)
Incredible String Band/Gently Tender
ISBN 1 899882 65 0 (£6.99)
Leonard Cohen/Came so Far for Love
ISBN 1 899882 50 2 (£5.99)
Captain Beefheart/Fast and Bulbous
ISBN 1 899882 25 1 (£5.99)
Arthur Lee/Love Story
ISBN 1 899882 60 X (£5.99)
Frank Zappa, Strictly Genteel Genius Rides Again
ISBN 1 899882 70 7 (£9.99)
My Generation, The Sixties Groups
ISBN 1 899882 80 4 (7.99)

Available from your local bookshop or direct from
Agenda Limited, Units 1 & 2, Ludgershall Business Park,
New Drove, Ludgershall, Andover, Hampshire, UK, SP11 9RN
We accept cheques-Eurocheques/registered cash, only in sterling.
Postage Free in UK/EEC, for R.O.W. add £1.50 per book.
Cheques payable to AGENDA LTD, please.
Sorry we do not accept credit cards.